# CLEANING
# HOUSE

## AMERICA'S CAMPAIGN
## FOR TERM LIMITS

*James K. Coyne and John H. Fund*

REGNERY GATEWAY
*Washington, D.C.*

Library of Congress Cataloging-In-Publication Data

Coyne, James K., 1946–
Cleaning house : America's campaign for term limits / James K.
Coyne and John H. Fund.
p.    cm.
Includes index.
ISBN 0-89526-516-8
1. United States. Congress—Term of office.   I. Fund, John H.,
1957–    .   II. Title.
JK1140.C69    1992
328.73'073—dc20                           92-19278
                                          CIP

Published in the United States by
Regnery Gateway
1130 17th Street, NW
Washington, DC 20036

Distributed to the trade by
National Book Network
4720-A Boston Way
Lanham, MD 20706

Printed on acid free paper

Manufactured in the United States of America

10  9  8  7  6  5  4  3  2  1

# CONTENTS

# ACKNOWLEDGEMENTS

THE TRUTH ABOUT political careerism hit me like a sledge-hammer.

It was at a political picnic in the late summer of 1982, one of the few opportunities I had that year to bring my whole family along with me on the campaign trail. A friendly television reporter approached us after we had spent a few hours chatting with constituents and swapping stories about our summer vacations and plans for the fall.

But she didn't want to talk to me. She had spotted our eldest son, Sandy, and hoped to continue a memorable interview she had had with him during our first congressional campaign, two years earlier. At the time, Sandy had just turned three and the reporter thought it would be cute to ask him a question.

"What do you want to be, when you grow up?" was her first query.

Sandy, a typically loquacious and unabashed little boy, responded quickly: "I'm going to be a scientist, a fireman, an astronaut, a baseball player, a daddy, and a congressman!"

That evening, we all joined him around the television as his remark was featured on the nightly news. We couldn't have been more proud.

Now the same reporter, along with her camera crew, was poised to repeat her interview with an older (now five years old) and wiser Sandy Coyne.

"What do you want to be when you grow up?" she asked, curious to see how Sandy's vocational ambitions had changed.

This time Sandy paused for just a second before responding: "I'd like to become a scientist, a fireman, an astronaut, a baseball player, and a daddy."

We all waited. Finally, the reporter asked, "But I thought you wanted to be a congressman, too?"

Sandy looked directly at the camera. "You can't be a daddy and a congressman," he declared.

That was the day I knew that congressional careerism was a disease. I'll never be able to thank Sandy enough for that insight.

He understood at the age of three that serving in Congress is something you're supposed to do along with all the other things that make up your life. It's not supposed to be your life.

I'm grateful to many others who have helped me see how Congress needs to be changed and how these changes should be presented in this book.

Former Representative Bill Frenzel, now with the Brookings Institution, was the first to share with me the truth about the bureaucratic inertia of the House. He also showed, by example, that it was possible to resist the corrupting influences of power, perquisites, and privilege.

I'm also deeply indebted to the many who have forged the intellectual underpinnings of the term limits movement, especially Ed Crane, president of the Cato Institute, Cleta Mitchell, director of the Term Limits Legal Institute, and Senator Hank Brown, the most outspoken proponent of term limits in the Senate.

Two others, Richard Willard and Charles Coyne (with the help of his daughter, Anna), donated valuable weekends to review our draft. Their suggestions were critical to the clarity and consistency of the final product. My friendship and indebtedness to them both knows no term limit.

Finally, I owe the deepest gratitude to my wife and dearest friend, Holly, who not only gave so much to this book, but has given me a life of happiness without limit. Our children,

Sandy, Kate, and Michael, have learned from her to listen to voices other than their own and to search for answers to questions that wait to be asked. To them, I give thanks for their patient support and understanding throughout this project, but also for the knowledge that the most important thing I can aspire to "when I grow up" is to be a good "daddy."

James K. Coyne
McLean, Virginia
1992

Not an Indian was in sight. The tiny island seemed deserted. Overhead in the cloudy sky, buzzards were circling. A drift of wind told him why; the air was heavy with the stench of rotting flesh.

As he was turning to ask Donovan if he was certain he had seen any of Forsyth's Scouts, his eyes caught a movement just below. A man had scurried out of a plum thicket and was running toward the island. Carpenter shouted at him, started his horse forward, and the others came on behind him at a fast trot.

Suddenly the man stopped, turned, and raised his carbine to take aim.

"Spread out! Wave your hats!" Carpenter commanded, and then bellowed at the man: "Don't shoot! We're friends!"

For a second the man remained frozen; then he tossed his carbine in the air and began cheering. Beyond him on the island, Carpenter saw other scouts crawling from their sand pits. Some were shouting, some running, some hobbling unsteadily. They looked like gaunt wolves.

Carpenter wondered if he had arrived too late to save his old friend, Sandy Forsyth.

# ACKNOWLEDGEMENTS

BOOKS ARE SUPPORTED before they are written. This effort would not have been possible without the financial support of Michael Joyce at the Bradley Foundation in Milwaukee and James Piereson of the John M. Olin Foundation. Both men have helped to enrich the climate of debate in this country more than they can imagine. The book would have remained random notes in a computer file if Bill Hammett of the Manhattan Institute had not agreed to provide the logistical help the project needed. He and Larry Mone saw the possibilities in this book and gave it the full support of the Institute.

I will always be grateful to friends who read portions of the manuscript and provided helpful advice, above all Ed Crane and David Boaz of the Cato Institute, both of whom saw the wisdom of term limits before almost anyone else I know. Melanie Kirkpatrick and Amity Shlaes, two valued colleagues of mine at the *Wall Street Journal*, helped me better frame and focus the arguments in the book.

This book would never have been possible if I had not had the opportunity to work at the editorial page of the *Wall Street Journal*, the most congenial and supportive workplace imaginable for someone who wants to examine and comment on issues of the day. Robert Bartley, the editor of the *Journal*, was convinced early on that term limits would be an important issue and allowed me to spend an inordinate amount of time delving into the topic. History will not fail to note his role in providing a forum for the modern term limit movement. Dan

Henninger, the deputy editor of the editorial page, vastly improved many of my articles on term limits for the *Journal*, some of which have been adapted for use in this book.

I am grateful to Alfred Regnery of Regnery Gateway, who was there every step of the way, and I appreciate the help of Megan Butler and Jennifer Reist at Regnery in making sure that all the pieces fit just so. The book benefited from having an editor as capable as Patricia Bozell.

This book was vastly improved by conversations with Tom Hazlett, Mark Petracca, Howard Rich, Ken Bode, Terry Considine, Lew Uhler, John Lewis, David Mason, Bob Hawkins, Mark Leidl, Tom Palmer, Elise Paylan, Ed Royce, John Barnes, Heather Richardson and Martin Wooster. Grover Norquist taught me more about politics than he will ever know. Vaclav Klaus and David Willetts provided me with European perspectives on the dangers of the political careerism they observed on trips to the United States. And, of course, I owe my parents more than I can ever say.

John H. Fund
New York, New York
1992

# Preface

# THE BEST JOB
# IN THE WORLD

IN THE SPRING of 1989, Americans watched in disgust as House Speaker Jim Wright was disgraced and forced to resign. Never before had a Speaker been caught with his hand in the cookie jar. A self-righteous Congress demanded that Jim Wright go.

Publicly, the House Ethics Committee declared that Jim Wright's sin was bending and even breaking the House rules against outside income, honoraria, and royalty income. He had been in cahoots with highrollers in Texas who furnished him with fancy cars, apartments, and cash, and the voters were further shocked to learn that lobbyists had bought thousands of copies of a thin volume of his recycled speeches to circumvent rules that forbade direct payments to members.

But the Ethics Committee whitewashed the most serious charges because they went to the heart of what today's Congress had become: it exonerated the Speaker for his strongarm tactics on behalf of insolvent Texas S&Ls. Wright had blocked legislation that would have closed them, even though some were run by crooks; he also had demanded special favors for various of the S&Ls and threatened regulators who wouldn't tow his line. When he couldn't get one regulator fired, Wright spread rumors that the man was gay. The Ethics

Committee claimed that though such actions were "intemperate," they were not "undue influence," and added that stigmatizing what the Speaker had done as improper would second-guess "the technique and personality of the legislator" and his efforts to help constituents. They didn't mention that it might also dry up one of the main wells of campaign contributions.

No, Wright's real sin in the minds of his fellow congressmen wasn't greed or interfering with regulators; it had nothing to do with ethics. It was that he hadn't been tough enough: he had caved in on the pay raise that was "automatically" being passed early in 1989. And many members who were frequently overdrawn at the House Bank desperately needed to have their $89,500 pay raised. Congressional leaders had rigged the pay raise bill to become law automatically, and it would have been if Wright had just kept his mouth shut and withstood the ridicule of an outraged nation.

But besieged by talk shows and voters, Wright's backbone buckled and he declared that he would survey the Congress and follow its lead. Of course, no member would admit openly that he wanted to sneak through the 50 percent raise, so the ploy failed and the carefully crafted pay grab had to be postponed a year.

Congress was livid. Speaker Wright was taking a dive.

Didn't he know that the real reason he had been chosen Speaker was to take the heat on tough votes like this? What was he thinking of, passing the buck right back to the members themselves!

From then on, Jim Wright no longer had the support of his party's rank and file, and they abandoned him two months later when the Ethics Committee charged him with feathering his own nest. To the members, it was fair play. Wright wouldn't stick his neck out for their pay raise, they wouldn't stick their necks out for him.

Wright, it seems, had misunderstood for whom he was

working, who had elected him to his high post, who controlled his empire. He was the Speaker, but the incumbents were King. And he paid the price.

Still, Wright did understand the first principle of congressional life. In a moment of prideful candor on his last day in office, he shared with the rest of us the thought that dominates every member's existence, defines his self-image, and motivates his political and private actions—he revealed the core truth of serving in Congress today.

A reporter for the *Washington Post* had staked him out one last time. She waited patiently in the ornate lobby outside his luxurious suite in the Capitol to catch him as he crossed the threshold of power the final time. As he walked by she asked, "What are your thoughts as you leave all this behind?"

"This is the best job in the world," he replied without hesitation. He no longer had to hide behind the usual platitudes about what a privilege it had been to serve, or how he'd tried to do what he thought was right, or how honored he'd been to represent the fine citizens of Forth Worth. He just told the truth—it's one helluva job!

Time and again you hear members of Congress confess that they've wanted to be congressmen for as long as they can remember. In Robert Cwiklik's recent biography of a freshman congressman, Peter Hoagland of Nebraska, we see the typical political sequence:[1]

Dreams in the seventh grade of a career in Congress; pursuit of all those "civic responsibility" resumé items in high school, college, and law school; a "people-oriented," i.e., ambulance-chasing, legal career that offers little satisfaction but builds up the bank account; apprenticeship in the local political vineyards and a decade or so of logrolling in the local legislature; and finally, when an open seat (never challenge an incumbent) appears, mortgaging the house, hitting up everyone who owed a favor, and spending a fortune on TV ads telling everyone what an "ordinary" and "experienced" fellow he was.

All the years leading up to Congress were just preparation, necessary seasons in the farm leagues waiting to be discovered—or waiting to get enough money to pay for your own political discovery. But finally you win; you have arrived.

For the professional politicians like Hoagland and Wright, election to Congress is a dream come true. Everything you feel about yourself is confirmed. You really are the best, the teacher's pet, the most likely to succeed, the one that will make it into the history books, the valedictorian for life, the home-town boy who made good—you're on top. As they say in the hair-coloring commercials, you're worth it.

The best job in the world, a dream come true—if you're not worth it, who is? But why stop at coloring your hair? Color everything you can! Spend everything you can! After all, it's other people's money. Get everything you can! Nothing's too good for you.

Of course, the fun has only just begun. Once you get to know it, Congress may remind you a little of a place where you spend several years and where you probably had a good time. It's a lot like high school, but this time with money. Being in Congress is like serving on your old high school council, only this time you have a trillion dollars to spend to impress your friends. You are under voter supervision, but the voters are indifferent and can easily be snowed. After all, they haven't caught on yet.

As you meet your freshmen classmates, you realize how much your colleagues remind you of the student cliques from school: the class grinds who sit up all night and read legisla-tion, the nerds who specialize in some arcane area of knowl-edge and can't talk about anything else, the jocks who are obsessed with being Big Men On Capitol Hill, the cheer-leaders who root mindlessly for one ideological cause or an-other, the hoods who police the membership and make sure no one breaks the code of silence by ratting to the voters, and the student body presidents who view Congress as a stepping-stone to bigger and better offices.

Congress is also much better than high school because, if you want, somebody else will do much of your studying for you. You are relieved of much of the responsibility for worrying about legislation by your attentive and knowledgeable staff. They are there, twenty-two of them in the House and up to eighty in the Senate, to do your bidding. You can ask them to work late without overtime, pick you up at the airport, work on your campaign in their spare time, anything you want. Congress has largely exempted itself from the minimum wage, fair labor practices, and antidiscrimination laws that cover every other employer in America. You are truly the Lord of your Incumbent Castle.

But as great a job as Congress is, a shadow has fallen over its future. The public has grown tired of seeing Congress accomplish little except shovel dubious pork-barrel spending out the door and perform regulatory favors for contributors. It no longer accepts all of the canned excuses about "divided government" and "complex issues"; it is demanding solutions to its concerns. Stories of congressional arrogance and hypocrisy have filtered back home. People openly complain about a Careerist Congress, full of time servers or political manipulators. Even voters who are grateful for the help they got clearing up that problem with Grandma's Social Security check are beginning to wonder if their own representative hasn't "gone native" in Washington and is now part of the problem instead of the solution.

This public dissatisfaction with Congress has had some effect on the 1992 election. A few more challengers are running, and they have a little more money. This time they may be outspent by only 4 to 1 instead of the usual 8 to 1. The revelations about check-kiting and no-interest loans at the House Bank have endangered some of Capitol Hill's high rollers. No doubt some incumbents with new postcensus territory will lose despite their best efforts to gerrymander their districts. But most members know that if they can ride through this rough year, they will be able to fine-tune their Incumbent Protection Machine and, absent another scandal, continue business pretty much as usual.

But another threat to the Careerist Congress may not go away so easily. All over the country, groups of citizen activists have banded together to fight not for a candidate, but for an ideal: the Citizen Legislature the Founding Fathers thought they were handing down to us. Their vehicle is term limitation, a ceiling on the number of years any one person can serve in a given office. The movement, barely three years old, has already made progress beyond anyone's expectations. Even some noted opponents of term limits say the idea has a good chance of becoming national policy by the end of this decade.

Career-oriented politicians despise term limits because these limits will radically alter their incentive structure. They will no longer be able to hang around in a safe seat until an opportunity for advancement opens. They will either have to try for promotion to another office or go back home to live with the consequences of the laws they enacted. A Citizen Legislature will of course have its share of professional politicians, but it will have more diverse members, members from backgrounds other than law or government. This new blood will be able to have greater impact, whether in Congress or in state legislatures, than before, and perhaps finally put an end to some of the log-rolling and mutual back-scratching that characterize the legislative process today.

Term limits are not a panacea. They will not address all the ills of our body politic. But they will effect a substantive and lasting change for the better in American government. That is why, unlike many other less substantive political reforms, they are fiercely opposed by the only organized political party America has—the Incumbent party.

In 1992, the Incumbent party has come up with a new

argument against term limits. Its adherents point to the record
number of members of Congress who are retiring this year
and say the system is correcting itself and doesn't need to be
changed. That's like saying that every time the system careens
out of control, it will smash into a tree, so you needn't worry.
"See!" its defenders point out. "It stopped! The system
worked!" We'd say the tree worked.

Any political system that requires a major scandal to change
its leadership is one that could use reforming. Voters can't
count on having a major scandal occur frequently enough to
act as an effective purging device. Besides, there's no way yet
of knowing how many incumbents will actually lose this fall
after they've fully revved up their reelection machines.

This book will tell the story of term limits from three major
perspectives. First, it will show how term limits are a popular
reaction to the perception that American democracy is a
closed system and under the excessive influence of careerists
and political professionals who often abuse their office, as Jim
Wright did. Second, it will show that term limits have a long
and honorable tradition in American political life dating back
to the Founders' deeply held belief in a Citizen Legislature.
And, last, it will show how term limits can be an important
means of reviving political competition and making legislators
more responsive to and representative of the people.

# CLEANING
# HOUSE

# 1

---

# TIME OUT FOR POLITICIANS

*Power tends to corrupt and absolute power corrupts absolutely.*

—LORD ACTON, 1887.

*The one pervading evil of democracy is the tyranny of the major-ity, or rather of that party, not always in the majority, that succeeds by force or fraud, in carrying elections.*

—LORD ACTON, 1907.

JANUARY 6, 1992, WAS a special day in the House of Represen-tatives for Jamie L. Whitten. That day the Mississippi Demo-crat became the longest-serving member in the history of the House, celebrating a marathon fifty years, two months, four-teen days as a representative. He had served 18,324 days with hardly a day lost to sickness. He had literally seen almost everything—his first election had taken place thirty-three days before Japanese bombs fell on Pearl Harbor.

The eighty-one-year-old Whitten celebrated his longevity quietly that day, holding court in his spacious suite of offices in the Rayburn Building. Scores of members called or stopped by to congratulate him, and gifts of flowers and bottles of spirits spilled into the hallway outside his office. Members and lobbyists had good reason to make certain that Whitten remembered their good wishes, for Jamie Whitten is no ordinary House member. In 1979 his seniority had conferred on him a position of unchallenged power and authority: chairmanship of the Appropriations Committee, which determines in minute detail how the U.S. government spends much of its money.

Whitten had joined the Appropriations Committee during his first term in office, determined to stay put and wait for the benefits of seniority. They began to pay off in 1949 when he became chairman of the Appropriations Subcommittee on Agriculture and Rural Development. He has held that position ever since, with the exception of 1953-55, the last time the Republicans controlled the House.

He has used that chairmanship to acquire legendary power. He is known as "the permanent secretary of agriculture," and stories about his vindictiveness and secretive nature abound on Capitol Hill. He has outlasted eight presidents and eighteen secretaries of agriculture, and has successfully blocked all of their efforts to reorient agricultural policy and move it away from the lavish subsidy programs of the New Deal. At his insistence, his own district and other rural areas continue to be showered with subsidy payments, soil preservation and reclamation programs, water projects, rural electrification, and highways.

And he has effectively crushed or scared off any political competition in his district. In the twenty-six elections in which he has been a candidate, he has faced an opponent only eleven times and never received less than 63 percent of the vote.

Whitten's legislative style is to play his cards close to his vest and divvy out pump-priming spending after consulting a small coterie of fellow legislators and lobbyists, and his power is seldom challenged. His subcommittee hearings are renowned for their brevity and the inarticulate mumblings of Mr. Whitten as he guides pork-barrel projects out the door. Whitten has no truck with the view that some conception of the common good should animate Congress. At the 125th anniversary of the Department of Agriculture in 1987 he bluntly told his audience that executive branch officials didn't appreciate the important role agriculture played in American life and were generally uninformed about the farm programs he and the rest of Congress had created. Mr. Whitten believes Congress's deliberations only decide which constituency will gain special advantage over others. His view of what modern government should be was succinct:

"Don't you see? All anyone ever wants is a special advantage over the next fellow. Understand that, and you've understood the intent of every law ever passed."[1]

That same year Whitten decided to flex his considerable power. In the early 1980s he had changed the way the Department of Agriculture's appropriations bill was handled. Before then it had been given one lump sum of money and he allowed the department to decide internally how it was spent. Instead, Whitten began micromanaging the budget of every under secretary and assistant secretary, dictating exactly how much and where they could spend money. In 1987, the assistant secretary for natural resources and the environment pulled out money for a dubious soil conservation program that was close to Whitten's heart. Whitten promptly yanked all funding for the office, effectively abolishing it.

In February 1992, Whitten's grasp on Appropriations Committee business weakened after he was hospitalized. When he returned, he was visibly frailer and less coherent. At a committee meeting in late April, he had difficulty understanding other members and frequently spoke while they were delivering their own statements. He was publicly urged by friends and colleagues to give up the chairmanship, but he refused: "I guess everything in life is possible, but this comes as close to being impossible as I could think of." When he was asked if anyone had suggested he step aside he retorted, "Anybody who says it to me, I'd question whether it was friendly advice they were giving me." As of July 1992, Mr. Whitten was still resisting efforts to limit his complete control of one of the most important committees in all of Congress.

It's hard to imagine that a career like Mr. Whitten's could occur outside of Congress. No company, save a small family firm, no university, no major foundation would keep someone in a powerful position continuously for nearly four decades.

In the executive branch, tenure stretching into decades is unheard of. The average cabinet secretary serves fewer than four years and the average assistant secretary in a cabinet department serves twenty-seven months. But many House and Senate members hang around endlessly.

Whitten is not the only powerful committee chairman. John Dingell, who has headed the Energy and Commerce Committee since 1981, has so successfully grabbed turf from other committee members that today 43 percent of all legislation is routed through his committee. "I swear," complained former Interior Committee Chairman Morris Udall, "that I think John employs some people on his staff whose only job is to poach legislation from other committees."

The kind of entrenched and expansive control over legislation that Jamie Whitten and John Dingell hold has led many Americans to call for an end to a Congress where long service has become a goal in itself because it translates into vast, often unchecked, power. That's why they have embraced the term limits movement.


The term limits movement may become the most interesting and debated political idea of the 1990s, but it didn't originate with politicians. It is directed at them. The move to restrict the tenure of officeholders has become what the tax revolt of the 1970s was—a popular movement that politicians despise, but one to which they must respond.

Indeed, not since California's Proposition 13 created a nationwide tidal wave of tax protest in the seventies has a political idea caught on with such speed. Polls show that over 75 percent of Americans support a limit on terms for elected officials. So far, states and cities where one out of every seven Americans lives, have voted some form of term limits into law in the last year alone. Over 145 bills to set term limits have already been introduced in forty-eight states, and term limits have became a major issue in the 1992 presidential campaign, with President George Bush, Pat Buchanan, Jerry Brown, and Paul Tsongas all endorsing the concept.

Still, the battle for term limits remains a populist and grass roots movement. Most elected officials continue to oppose them, especially when a concrete proposal is made in *their* state. The gulf between legislators and the American people has never been greater than on this issue. Surveys show a solid majority of elected officials opposing term limits, even when they themselves are grandfathered into office. A Gallup survey in 1990 interviewed 158 U.S. House members and 302 state legislators; it found that 66 percent of the House members and 59 percent of the state legislators opposed limiting their terms of office. When in 1991 the Senate conducted a roll call vote on term limits, it lost 67 to thirty-one.

At the same time, the notion is overwhelmingly popular with Americans, regardless of party, ideology, or income. Indeed it sweeps all demographic groups. Blacks favor it even more than whites, women more than men. No issue, even the death penalty, commands such a broad base of support. Martin Plissner, political director of CBS News, says he has "never seen an issue on which there was so little demographic variation."[2]

Term limits were a part of the nation's first governing document, the Articles of Confederation, but were left out of the Constitution largely because it was thought of as "entering too much into detail" for a short document. Nonetheless, self-imposed limits on officeholders were long a part of America's public service ethic; members of Congress returned to private life after two or three terms. With the rise of larger government, term limitation, once the accepted American tradition, has been replaced by congressional careerism. That is why many Americans now believe that limitations must be made part of the nation's laws.

Term limitation is not a new idea. It applies today to twenty-eight governors along with innumerable mayors, city council members, and, of course, the president of the United States. Over the years, term limits for Congress have been endorsed by the likes of Thomas Jefferson, Abraham Lincoln, Harry Truman, Dwight Eisenhower, and John F. Kennedy.[3] Many former state legislators also believe the idea should be extended to state legislatures, now that most of them have switched from being part-time bodies of citizen legislators to full-time professional entities.

In the space of just eighteen months, the term limits concept has moved from being an esoteric political science topic to a nationwide movement. In passing term limits, advocates have had to overcome opposition from almost every element of the political establishment—from elected officials to the major news media. Yet they have lost only one major election.

In 1990, three states—Oklahoma, Colorado, and California—limited their state legislators' terms, with Colorado also limiting its congressional delegation. Term limits have also been approved for local officials in many American cities. The record of all term limits that have been passed by voters to date:

San Francisco, June 1990 (64 percent in favor; limits county supervisors to eight years in office)

Oklahoma, September 1990 (67 percent in favor; limits state legislators to twelve years total service in both houses)

California, November 1990 (52 percent in favor; limits all statewide officials to two four-year terms along with state senators, limits state assemblymen to three two-year terms)

Colorado, November 1990 (71 percent in favor; limits state-

wide officials and members of the legislature to eight
years in office)

San Jose, California, November 1990 (57 percent in favor;
retroactive limit to two four-year terms)

Kansas City, Missouri, November 1990 (57 percent in favor;
retroactive, eight-year limit)

Wichita, Kansas, February 1991 (52 percent in favor; eight-
year limit)

Colorado Springs, Colorado, April 1991 (67 percent in favor; eight-year limit)

San Antonio, Texas, May 1991 (65 percent in favor; four-
year limit)

Jacksonville, Florida, May 1991 (82 percent in favor; six-
year limit)

New Orleans, Louisiana, October 1991 (68 percent in favor;
eight-year limit)

Cincinnati, Ohio, November 1991 (59 percent in favor;
eight-year limit)

Houston, Texas, November 1991 (59 percent in favor; six-
year limit)

Worcester, Massachusetts, November 1991 (74 percent in
favor; an advisory initiative on limiting terms of office for
city, state, and federal officials)

Rockville, Maryland, November 1991 (59 percent in favor;
eight-year limit)

Palo Alto, California, November 1991 (58 percent in favor;
eight-year limit)

Texas, March 1992 (82 percent registered Republicans in
favor of an advisory referendum; similar vote attempted
in the Democratic primary, but that party's state executive
committee refused to put it on the ballot)

Term limits have lost twice at the polls; and one of those
hardly counts. An unappealing term limits measure lost in
White Plains, N.Y., in November 1991 because voters viewed it

as settling a political score. Republican Mayor Alfred Del Vecchio, whose charter revision panel had proposed the amendment, was at odds with the Democratic majority on the city council. The proposal would have limited the council to eight years in office, but imposed no limit on the mayor. Mr. Del Vecchio had already served sixteen years in office. Voters recognized this for the political ploy it was and rejected the term limit with 64 percent of the vote

The more serious loss occurred in Washington State, where a proposal for a very strict term limit on state and federal officials lost 54 percent to 46 percent in November 1991 because of structural flaws. Unlike most others, the Washington limit was retroactive, and would have kicked out Speaker Tom Foley and the rest of the congressional delegation in three years. Many voters concluded that the state could ill afford to lose so much clout so quickly. A less extreme limit, or one passed simultaneously with several other states, would have passed.[4]

Term limits initiatives will be on fifteen state ballots this fall, including California, Florida, Michigan, Ohio, Oregon, South Dakota, and Wyoming. All of these initiatives will seek to apply term limits to the congressional delegations of their respective states.

Article I, Section 8 of the Constitution forbids the granting of any titles of nobility, but given the lifetime tenure of congressmen, we might as well have dukes and barons in Congress, claims Pete du Pont, former House member and governor of Delaware. Indeed, the 7 percent annual turnover in Britain's nonelected House of Lords, where vacancies only occur through death, was just below the average turnover in the House of Representatives until the rash of retirements in 1992. The House is no longer representative of the people.

The present-day powers of incumbency have become a shield protecting members of Congress from competition. In recent years, it's become almost impossible to throw the rascals out. In 1988, only six of the 405 House members lost their elections, and five of those incumbents were under some ethical cloud. In 1990, 96.2 percent of incumbents won. Of the sixteen unlucky losers, about half had ethical problems. Four out of five incumbents won in 1990 with over 60 percent of the vote. Four Senate incumbents and 69 House members had no major party opposition. Finding good challengers to run against most incumbents is like recruiting pilots for kamikaze missions. How many of the readers of this book would try it?

It is true that a large number of incumbents may lose in the 1992 elections because they wrote bad checks at the House Bank, causing an unprecedented level of voter disgust. But how long will that outrage last? Without term limits, incumbents are likely to win overwhelming reelection in any year that doesn't have a megascandal. PAC money will no doubt continue to flood incumbents; few special interests want to anger those members who will decide the fate of their legislation. In 1990, PACs gave $117 million to House and Senate incumbents and only $15.6 million to challengers. The country cannot afford to wait another twenty years for its next House-cleaning.

The entrenched incumbency of Congress is, moreover, trickling down to the state legislative level. In the 1960s and 1970s typically one-third of the membership of state legislatures changed every two years. In earlier decades turnover rates of 50 percent were common. In the 1980s turnover slowed to a crawl, and in 1988 an all-time low of only 16 percent of state legislators were newly elected. In 1990 the number rose slightly to 20 percent.

In California, the state with the professionalized legislature that most resembles Congress, only seven incumbents lost in the last three legislative elections before the passage of term limits. More than 365 won. The turnover rate for assembly members had dropped by half since 1980. Now, with term

limits, over one-fourth of the legislators are retiring or running for other offices.

In New York, only eight of 211 legislators chose not to run
in 1990. Only six of the 203 incumbents who ran were defeated. Over 86 percent of the state's legislators hold a "safe
seat," defined as a winning margin of more than 20 percentage points. In Pennsylvania, 98 percent of incumbents in the
state legislature won reelection in 1988 and 1990.

Critics say the trend is even seeping down to the local level.
"Entrenched incumbency is strangling local government and
the quality of life is suffering in many ways," notes Professor
Laura Lake of the University of California at Los Angeles.[5]

Term limits work for many occupations in America. Why
not for legislators? Presidents are limited, twenty-eight of the
nation's fifty governors are limited, executive branch employees are limited, and nearly everyone in the private sector
faces pressure to honor a "term limitation" of some kind—"65
and out," or whatever—no matter how respected, important,
or powerful they are.


More and more voters no longer participate in elections. Those
that do are increasingly mad at the system. So why do most of
them still vote for the only person on the ballot they know: the
incumbent? First, many members have convinced voters they
are no longer primarily responsible for national policy but
should instead be viewed as glorified ombudsmen. For that
part of their job, many members still receive high marks.

Second, people will not vote for an unknown challenger who
can not even raise enough money to force the media to notice
his existence. According to Common Cause, the nonpartisan
lobby, of the 406 House incumbents seeking reelection in
1990, 79 had no major party opposition. Another 218—a
majority of the entire House—had opponents who raised less
than $25,000, and 86 others had opponents who raised more

than $25,000 but less than half the amounts the incumbents raised. Only 25 races were remotely competitive. Voters who only know the incumbent, won't turn Mr. Big out of office if his only opponent is Mr. Nobody.

Until the House Bank scandal scrambled the political deck for this one election, incumbents could stay as long as they wanted. Only scandal, sloppy delivery of constituent services, or a demographically changing district could pose real threats to their tenure.

The day a new House member arrives on Capitol Hill, he is given the "perk book." Officially called the *Congressional Handbook*, its four-hundred pages are packed with useful information about how to send millions of letters to constituents free of charge, how to spend generous travel and office allowances, how to hire up to twenty-two paid staffers to polish their image and do favors for constituents, and how to bring home the bacon in the form of federal grants to the district. Mobile offices in the district can keep them in constant touch with even isolated voters. Members can set up twenty-four hour constituent hot lines. Never mind small ethical dilemmas, you will get reelected anyway, the book seems to say.

Members have become increasingly savvy at courting the media. The number of House press secretaries has gone up five times since 1970. Overworked reporters rely on them heavily for information on Congress. Take Rep. Bill Lowery, a Republican from San Diego, California, who had a safe seat until he was forced to retire in the wake of the S&L and House Bank scandals. His press secretary Tina Kreischer was so successful in pushing her boss's point of view that she estimates at least 75 percent of the stories about him in the *San Diego Union*, the district's largest newspaper, were based on her press releases. Former reporter Mark Ragan, who covered Capitol Hill for the *Union*, reports that the bureau relied on Lowery handouts "heavily." "They're all so busy," he said. "Tina was very helpful."[6]

Television reporters also get a lot of attention from congressional press secretaries. Use of the House's in-house broadcast studio has quadrupled in the last decade, partly because it offers members bargain rates some 60 percent below commercial studios. Video press releases churned out by congressional offices often end up on local TV stations, and a *Washington Journalism Review* survey found that 87 percent of stations rarely advise viewers when the "news" footage they see comes from a congressional office.[7]

Those who know Congress well have often wondered how to explain the bizarre culture of Capitol Hill to the average American. Robert Bartley, editor of the *Wall Street Journal*, suggests that Congress resembles nothing so much as an alien universe:

> Imagine that Captain Kirk and the starship *Enterprise* trekked to the third planet of an ordinary star in an obscure arm of the Milky Way. And imagine that they discovered that the most important nation there was ruled by 535 elders, elected in their youth to life terms. Well, perhaps not quite life. Elders were permitted to resign if overcome by a sense of meaninglessness, a not uncommon occurrence. And in extraordinary circumstances, say a second offense of sexual abuse, social pressure would force them to stand down.
>
> Once anointed, of course, elders were expected to take up life at court. Their only obligation was to visit the territory from which they had been elected every two or six years, depending on their rank, to go through the formality of reanointment. While not given great wealth if they did not already have it, they were provided with everything wealth could buy: marble palaces, large staffs of retainers to do their bidding, and most of all the expectation of deference by lesser humans. They could summon and bully commercial titans or certified scientific ge-

niuses, for example. And, of course, their enterprises were
immune from the laws that bound common citizens.

There were intrigues and disputes among the elders, but
these were resolved by subtle systems of social controls: those
who defied the sacred consensus were ostracized as trouble-
makers, particularly if they gave voice to plebeian objections to
the provisions for or commanded by elders. This curious system
called itself government of the people, by the people, and for
the people. Searching the anthropological tapes, Mr. Spock
classified it as an elected aristocracy.[8]

Bartley's view is, we submit, a chillingly accurate portrayal of
the modern Congress. While we pay homage to the ideas of
Madison and Jefferson in our schools, we have over time developed a political class with its own interests and its own agenda.
As Virginia Governor Douglas Wilder, a Democrat, puts it:
"Our two-party system is becoming a competition between the
party inside Washington and that new party, the vast majority
of Americans who live outside."[9]

Evidence in a few cases shows that America's ruling class is
becoming hereditary. George Bush is the son of a U.S. senator
and far more a creature of Washington than a citizen of his
adopted state of Texas. John Dingell, the "chairmonster" of
the House Energy and Commerce Committee, was first elected in 1955. His father had held the seat for twenty-three years
before that, and no doubt the current Representative Dingell
will be replaced by his son, now a state senator, or by his wife,
the well-connected General Motors lobbyist, Debbie Dingell.
George Miller was elected congressman from California from
1945 to 1972. His son has occupied the same seat for the last
eighteen years. Even daughters are getting into the act. When
Guy Molinari, a New York Republican, resigned to take a local
office, he handed the seat to his thirty-year-old daughter,
Susan.

The children of members don't always wait until their parents retire to work on Capitol Hill. In 1967, after the public

discovered that fifty members had their wives on the congressional payroll, Congress passed a law prohibiting any member from hiring a relative to work in his office. But "loophole nepotism" is still alive and well on Capitol Hill—at least eighty congressional relatives have worked on Capitol Hill in the last two years. No restrictions apply if relatives work for Congress itself or for other members.

Some, it seems, are quite willing to make Congress a family business:

When Massachusetts Rep. Joseph Early's nephew, Dennis, left a $26,000-a-year job with Rep. Bob Traxler in 1986, it was Representative Early's son, Mark, who replaced him. Representative Traxler also hired Stacey AuCoin, the daughter of Rep. Les AuCoin, as an office aide.

Representative AuCoin's brother, Leland, in turn works for the House clerk. Representative AuCoin has also provided paid internships for the daughters of Reps. Barbara Boxer and Carroll Hubbard. An AuCoin aide says it is "common practice" for members to employ "the kids of other congressmen."

The wife of Rep. Tom Downey (D.-N.Y.), one of the worst abusers of the House Bank, worked as an auditor for the House Bank. The office of the House Sergeant-at-Arms denied that Nancy Downey had any direct, day-to-day duties at the bank, but several customers frequently saw her working on the bank's records.

This kind of hiring isn't illegal, and most such employees are undoubtedly capable and hardworking. But certainly questions can be raised about some of them. Such as the wife of Rep. Charles Rose who, UPI reported in 1989, often showed up for work on an Agriculture subcommittee chaired by her husband in jogging clothes. She is said to be there hardly enough "to get her telephone messages."

The cost of employing a few relatives is small potatoes to people in a town where Office of Management and Budget computers don't kick in unless congressional budget items exceed

$100,000. But the public nonetheless has a right to be outraged. So do executive branch employees. The Beltway is a place where administration officials are expected to avoid even "the appearance" of a conflict of interest. A few years ago, reports that the U.S. Information Agency had hired the children of a few Reagan appointees had Congress and the media in a tizzy. Within weeks almost all of the kin were employed elsewhere.

Mark Twain once lampooned the kind of double standard Congress luxuriates in when he quipped, "To do good is noble. To advise others to do good is also noble, and much less trouble." Congress clearly does not want to be troubled with anything but directing the behavior of others.


Members who leave Congress are often struck at how different the real world is from life at the royal court of Washington. Donald Rumsfeld, a former congressman and secretary of defense, says that today, as a major corporate executive, he is ashamed at how little attention he paid in office to the problems of the private sector. George McGovern, a senator for eighteen years and the 1972 Democratic presidential candidate, bought a hotel in Connecticut in 1988. "I wish I had known a little more about the problems of the private sector," he told the *Washington Post*. "I have to pay taxes, meet a payroll—I wish I had had a better sense of what it took to do that when I was in Washington."

Even savvy political players are surprised at how out of touch Congress is after they come into direct contact with it. Richard Phelan was an active Democrat and national convention delegate for Sen. Paul Simon when in 1988 he was named special counsel to the House Ethics Committee to investigate Speaker James Wright. The next year, after Speaker Wright had been forced to resign under an ethical cloud, Phelan returned to Chicago with a new appreciation of what is wrong with Washington: "In 1988, all but one of the incumbents who chose to run and were defeated had ethical problems. Now that says to me that with the franking privilege, the PACs, all of the other people had been scared off or weren't able to raise enough money. What we now have is a House of Lords instead of a popularly elected Congress. . . It's difficult, if not impossible, for members not to be reelected to it. I think that carries with it a great deal of problems. Lots and lots of people have suggested to me that one of the things Congress ought to do is to limit their own terms."[10]

There are powerful reasons for both liberals and conservatives to endorse term limits. For conservatives there is overwhelming evidence that the longer politicians stay in office, the more committed they are to expanding government. James Miller, director of the Office of Management and Budget under President Reagan, has examined congressional spending patterns and found that members who serve the longest have significantly higher spending scores. In every year from 1978 to 1990, members of the House of Representatives who had served fewer than twelve years were more fiscally conservative than those who had served longer, based on National Taxpayers Union ratings. This pattern held true regardless of political party: senior Republicans, like senior Democrats, were more pro-spending than their junior counterparts.

James Payne, a budget scholar, found that representatives and senators who had been in office for more than twelve years made the difference in passing the 1990 budget summit agreement that socked Americans with the largest five-year tax increase in history. In the Senate, the budget passed by nine votes, but with senior senators excluded it would have failed 26 to 32. In the House, the budget package passed by twenty-eight votes, but without the votes of senior members it would have failed 142 to 146. Of the twenty-five members in competitive races, only five voted for the budget deal. The lack of competitive districts cost the American people right where it counts—in their wallet.[11]

Liberals also have strong reasons to come out for term limits. Ralph Nader, the consumer activist, says that "as public service becomes a highly paid career, rather than a civic duty to be briefly and effectively rendered, legislators solicit job security from wealthy special interests who can finance campaigns and defeat opponents. The needs of voters soon are replaced by the wants of corporate lobbies." Nader thinks term limits are needed to "end the long-standing alliances between special interest groups and individual legislators with campaign-financed lifetime tenures, the arrangement that has paralyzed legislature after legislature and the Congress."[12]

Cleta Deatherage Mitchell, a former Democratic legislator from Oklahoma, compares members of Congress today to the noncustodial parent in a divorced family: they visit on weekends and on holidays, they send money. "But they don't live with us, and over time they become mere acquaintances rather than people who really know their constituents."[13]

Last year, two remarkable books made the bestseller lists. One, by E. J. Dionne of the *Washington Post*, was called *Why Americans Hate Politics*. The other was P. J. O'Rourke's riotously funny *Parliament of Whores*. Those titles sum up the feelings of many voters. Americans are not suffering from political apathy. Instead, as a study by the Kettering Foundation found, they are angry about politics. They feel the democratic process has been hijacked by a closed group of career politicians who respond to the wishes of special interests rather than individual citizens. Voters haven't dropped out of politics—they've been pushed out of it.

The Kettering Foundation assembled a cross-section of Americans in ten cities to probe their attitudes on politics. Kettering concluded that most Americans still have a strong sense of civic duty but feel helpless to change a process they view as a closed system controlled by politicians, lobbyists, and the media.[14]

The view most voters in the Kettering study had of politicians was bitter and cynical. Many people are committing their civic time and energy to their local communities where they think they can make a difference. At the national and even state level, people equate politics with leprosy: they don't want to be around it.

"Policymakers are speaking a different language," a Richmond, Virginia, man said. "It's one of avoidance; it's one of 'it needs further study.' " A Philadelphia woman believes that while many people enter politics with good intentions, "they get caught up in the system and eventually just blend in."

"Congress has gone haywire," asserted Sen. Kent Conrad, a forty-four-year-old Democrat from North Dakota who is retiring this year. "People know that Congress isn't working, but they don't know why, or where to turn for answers."[15]

This doesn't mean citizens don't believe problems shouldn't be addressed. Many of them are in fact taking matters into their own hands. Millions of Americans are involved in community and neighborhood associations. Volunteerism and charitable giving are thriving. People are now willing to get involved, but only if they see the possibility of forward movement—which they don't see coming from Washington. "Community involvement brings about change, politics doesn't," says a Dallas man. A generation after the Great Society, more and more Americans are rediscovering the Jeffersonian ideals of community—local government and individual responsibility.

Reformers in Washington frequently call for campaign-finance reform as a way to reduce influence-peddling and enhance political competition. But they must realize that members of Congress change the finance laws. Bill Frenzel, a former Minnesota congressman and present resident scholar at the Brookings Institution, says he supports term limits because he can't believe Congress will ever pass campaign-finance reform that will defang the special interests and give challengers an even break against the incumbents who write the laws.

In addition, the influence of money on politics is merely a symptom of the underlying problem: the government's growing power to determine economic outcomes—subsidies, loans, protection against competition, the defense pork barrel, entitlements. Washington, that is, decides who benefits. The late Nobel laureate F. A. Hayek explained the process more than forty years ago: "As the coercive power of the state will alone decide who is to have what, the only power worth having will be a share in the exercise of this directing power."

The quest for that power has made Washington a boom town, filled with trendy boutiques and expense account restaurants. As the potential for political profit increases, the ranks of those seeking them—the ultimate insider traders—swell.

The Washington lawyer's bar has more than 46,000 members, double the number in 1976. In 1971, New York City had twice as many trade associations as Washington. Today, the names of 3,100 associations clog the Washington phone book, far outstripping New York. They employ more than eighty thousand people, and their top executives earn an average of $125,000. A fantastic 65 percent of the CEOs of Fortune 200 companies visit Washington at least once every two weeks. In the early 1970s fewer than 15 percent did. As long as a powerful government has enough favors to auction off, the special-interest bidding war will continue.

The late Sen. Paul Douglas of Illinois, one of the most revered figures ever to serve on Capitol Hill, warned of the pressure of groups, customers, clients, and claimants of the government that put their "most aggressive foot forward and sometimes seem not to scruple where or on whom they step. Officialdom is in time conditioned by the very forces with which it contends. A society which produces only unrestrained pressures on government cannot for long produce officials who will be able to resist those pressures."[16]

Certainly, the kind of people elected to Congress today are unlikely to be able to resist those pressures. As Alan Ehrenhalt learned in his pathbreaking book, *The United States of Ambition*, a new class of professional politicians with ambition, "talent," and a willingness to say or do whatever it takes to get elected has taken over electoral politics at both the congressional and, increasingly, the state level. This "permanent government" of professionals is more skilled at working the levers of influence than its predecessors; its "talent" is getting and staying elected.

If individually talented, collectively these egocentric members of Congress produce an "inept" Congress. Teamwork is rare, camaraderie is a luxury, hypocrisy is commonplace, national goals are ignored. Because their self-image and careers are wrapped up in holding office, they take few risks. "The more a person's career, livelihood and self-image depend on remaining in office, the more likely he is to magnify the smallest threat to that office," writes Mr. Ehrenhalt. That explains why members who hold ever safer seats become ever more cowardly and biddable to the powerful special interests from whom they get campaign dollars. As small as the chance of losing is, they can't afford to risk derailing their careers.

As they climb the seniority ladder in Congress, those tendencies become exacerbated. "Experience in government tends to produce legislators who are more interested in defending their turf than they are in solving serious public problems," says Mark Petracca, an assistant professor of politics at the University of California at Irvine. Petracca has traced the origin of term limits to the works of Aristotle, who first advocated "rotation in office" as a means by which the use of public office for private gain could be limited. Aristotle and other philosophers valued rotation in office because it meant that public officials would be both "the ruled and the rulers in turn."

The emergence of political careerists has led to what the Cato Institute's Ed Crane calls a "culture of ruling" in Washington. Members are constantly surrounded by flatterers trying to influence them in some way. It is enough to make even the most moral people change. And change they do.

Leo McCarthy, now lieutenant governor of California, was once asked by an aide what the difference was between how he felt when he was first elected as a lowly state legislator and now as the second-highest official in the state. He reported that when he was first elected to office he would walk into a room full of people in his district and proudly think, "I am the most important person in this room." Years later, after having become entrenched in office, he would walk into a room full of people and think, "I am the most important person who has EVER been in this room."

Once politicians become comfortable with the culture of ruling, many decide they don't ever want to leave it. So they begin voting themselves the means to guarantee their reelection and digging defensive moats against outsiders who want to enter the system.

The main job of Congress is to legislate solutions to the nation's problems, or if that is asking too much, to stay the hell out of the way and not make the problem worse. Unfortunately, members of Congress have largely abdicated their legislative responsibilities to become errand boys and grant makers. Legislators tend to concentrate today on the constituent casework and creation of federal programs that help win them elections. The longer members serve in Congress, the better they become at getting favors for favored constituents.

Congress does less and less, yet it is seemingly in session all the time. Former Rep. Thomas Curtis of Missouri points out that there is still a law on the books that Congress must adjourn no later than July 31 of each year except in times of war or a national emergency. Since World War II, it has complied with that law only twice.

Congress uses all of its extra meeting time in passing a great deal of legislation, but much of it is frivolous. Of the 240 public laws passed in 1989, nearly half were feel-good legislation—commemorative bills celebrating such things as National Tap Dance Day, National Job Skills Week, Federal Employees Recognition Week, and National Digestive Disease Awareness Month. The 95th Congress, during the Carter era, passed thirty-four such laws; the 101st Congress passed nearly three hundred.

But when it comes to laws of real substance, Congress ducks its responsibility. In 1990, it passed the extremely vague Americans with Disabilities Act and left it to federal agencies to write the specific rules that must be obeyed. Rulemaking steps on toes—the reason Congress avoids it in the first place, which then allows members to turn around and berate the agencies if they write rules their constituents complain about. "Congressmen get the laws they want because ultimately agencies almost always write the rules the way that congressional staff tells them to," declares Eric Felten, who is writing a book on Congress's abdication of its legislative responsibility. "As a bonus, a member often can collect a campaign contribution from a grateful constituent who doesn't realize that Congress is to blame in the first place for the problem he had."[17]

To keep all this wheel-spinning in motion Congress has had to take on more hired help. Since 1961, when John F. Kennedy was president, the number of congressional staffers who work directly for House and Senate members has nearly tripled, from 5,800 in Kennedy's day to over fifteen thousand today. Congress is now a Fortune 500-size employer. Staffers make up an unelected subgovernment, writing legislation their bosses seldom completely understand, micromanaging federal agencies, and launching investigations of whatever suits them. Unlike their bosses, they are almost completely unregulated by conflict-of-interest laws and often accept large speaking fees and junkets from entities with an interest in legislation. When World War II ended, it only cost $54 million to run all of Congress. Today the price tag is nearly $2.5 billion.

"Committee chairmen often have the power of potentates, not lawmakers. Staffers often serve as lawmakers, and much of the constituent work done by Congress today is properly the role of the executive branch," notes Larry Hansen, who served as administrative assistant to former Democratic Sen. Adlai Stevenson in the late 1970s.[18]

Mr. Hansen recalls that Mark Twain pointed out that "Public opinion is held in reverence. It settles everything. Some think it is the voice of God." Mr. Hansen quips that the record of Congress in recent years "suggests that many members have stopped listening—to the public, their better natures, and perhaps even to God."

Term limits are not likely to be passed by the current Congress. The heady atmosphere of Capitol Hill is enough to turn even the most populist member into a defender of congressional turf.

Utah Rep. James Hansen was an outspoken believer in term limits when he was first elected in 1980. He told reporters that he would be "the biggest hypocrite in the world" to support term limits and not leave office. But when reminded of his statement as he geared up to run for a seventh term in 1992, Hansen denied ever making it. He said he would be putting Utah at a disadvantage if he didn't run because the state would lose his valuable seniority.

Another supporter of term limits who changed his mind once he had spent time inside the Beltway is Rep. Joel Hefley, a Republican from Colorado. He was elected in 1986 on a platform that supported term limits. When he first got to Washington he introduced a term limits constitutional amendment.

Now, settled in a secure seat, he calls term limits "un-American" and says voters should be "smart enough to see through all" the self-promotion and advantages of incumbency. "I did not come to Washington to take away the people's democratic choices. The best term limit is the one we have right now: elections," he declares.

Such arguments ignore the fact that voters have little choice at the polls. That's one reason voter turnout has fallen from 48 percent in the 1966 congressional elections to 32 percent today. Remember, too, that the Constitution is filled with limitations on democracy, as befits America's republican form of government. The Constitution restricts the president to two terms, establishes a minimum age requirement for the president (35), and for members of the Senate (30) and House (25). Laws limiting the right to vote to citizens who have been residents of their area for a time and who are not convicted felons are common at the state level.

"The net effect of these limitations is not to reduce but to enhance the efficient functioning of the political system," notes James Davidson, chairman of the National Taxpayers Union. "Term limits would allow more genuine choice at the polls than we have today."[19]

Congress routinely excludes itself from all the regulatory laws it passes. The nearby box lists some of the landmark laws everyone in America must obey—except Congress. Employees of Congress are denied health and safety protections, collective-bargaining rights, and the right to sue for anti-discrimination damages in a federal court. Several years ago an air quality inspector tried to serve Congress's Capitol power plant with a violation notice. The manager of the plant sent the inspector packing, asserting that Congress had exempted itself from the Clean Air Act.

Members defend such exemptions by arguing that Congress has a right to manage its internal affairs and that they must be given complete freedom to hire and fire employees.

## ABOVE THE LAW

Congress does not live by the same laws you do. Here are fifteen laws Congress chose to exempt itself from:

Civil Rights Restoration Act of 1988
Ethics in Government Act of 1978
Age Discrimination Act Amendments of 1975
Privacy Act of 1974
Rehabilitation Act of 1973
Title 9 of Higher Education Amendments of 1972
Equal Employment Opportunity Act of 1972
Occupational Safety and Health Act of 1970
Age Discrimination Act of 1967
Freedom of Information Act of 1966
Civil Rights Act of 1964
Equal Pay Act of 1963
Minimum Wage Act of 1938
National Labor Relations Act of 1935
Social Security Act of 1933

No one questions that a member has to be able to hire a staff that is both loyal and compatible. But why should voters have to accept the blanket hypocrisy of a legislative body saddling private citizens and businesses with burdensome regulations from which it exempts itself?

When Sen. Charles Grassley of Iowa tried to apply the Civil Rights Bill to Congress in 1990, he was told by Sen. Warren Rudman, "This is the United States Senate. We are not your local manufacturer." Rudman added, "It is absolutely essential that, as to our legislative employees, we have an absolute right without outside review by anyone of what we do." To do anything else would only encourage "frivolous lawsuits"—no doubt the kind that ordinary businesses have to face, and often have to settle, every day.

Senate Majority Leader George Mitchell became almost

beet red when a proposal was made to apply the Occupational Safety and Health Act to Congress in 1991. "This is the most blatantly, flagrantly, obviously unconstitutional proposal I've seen since I've been in the Senate," he shouted, and went on to fulminate about "this phony argument that we ought to be treated like everybody else." Lawrence Tribe, a professor at the Harvard Law School, disagrees. He believes it is "simply wrong to see any serious separation of powers or speech-and-debate-clause problem" in forcing Congress to live by the laws it passes for others.

"Congress would exempt itself from the laws of gravity if it could," says Rep. Henry Hyde of Illinois. He warns that by writing exemptions from laws for itself, Congress is undermining its moral authority to legislate rules for the rest of society.

The culture of ruling has contributed to an ethically adrift Congress that lurches from one scandal to another—Jim Wright's infamous "junk book," the midnight pay raise, one thousand-page continuing resolutions, exemptions from the law, Tony Coelho's S&L loans, the Keating Five, the Clarence Thomas hearings, the House Bank, and the House Post Office. Congress almost seems hell-bent on doing the wrong thing time and time again. And it is largely oblivious to the appearance of its actions; it engages in ritual acts of denial that its behavior falls outside the accepted norms of society. One could almost be excused for thinking that all this is not by accident. It's almost as if members know what a mess Congress has become, but they just can't bring themselves to admit it and do something about it. The irrational and self-destructive behavior of Congress might even be viewed as a silent cry for help by its members: "Stop us before we run again!" We agree. It's time for the tough love of term limits.

# 2

## MEMBERSHIP HAS ITS PRIVILEGES

**mem·ber**, *noun: a person belonging to an incorporated or organized body, society, etc.; as, a member of a club, a member of Congress.*

FEW PEOPLE CALL IT organized. To many, it looks like a club. Whatever it is, Congress has its privileges.

Americans everywhere seem consumed with the privileges of membership. Fashionable blouses and jackets are emblazoned with the mysterious brand "Members Only." Country club membership requirements become issues of national debate. The American Express card disingenuously calls its customers "members" and brags about their benefits. We all, it seems, have to belong to something—and whatever it is, it must have its privileges.

It's not surprising, then, that Congress, our nation's most exclusive club, should be the paradigm of privilege. Tired of "being an example" to our nation's young, weary of displaying traditional values like virtue, industry, or humility, its members have enthusiastically embraced their new duty as America's role-models for receiving favors, indulgences, dispensations, and perquisites. Our citizens, they must assume, need some-

29

one to look (up? down?) to for guidance in acceptable levels of greed, a mirror for the me-generation.

We should be happy, therefore, that our senators and representatives take this aspect of their jobs so seriously. Their pursuit of creative forms of gratuity supports an army of professional panderers, promotes the growth of such key economic sectors as travel, entertainment, and recreation, and establishes America as a leader in an important and growing area of professional skill. We're lucky to have these "perk-aholics" who selflessly devote so much of their time to the pursuit of political privilege.

Who would have imagined, thirty years ago, that new electoral power and technology could create the marvels of political plunder we take for granted today: schedules that provide a dozen free vacations each year; travel around the globe on taxpayer-financed private jets; free use of vacation homes, yachts, and plush penthouses; to say nothing of nightly wining and dining in America's new culinary capital, Washington, D.C.

One of the least-known perks is the ability members have to pay some personal expenses out of their campaign funds. Rep. Bill Alexander, an Arkansas Democrat who was among the twenty-two top abusers of the House Bank, paid $28,638 in personal expenses out of his campaign account in 1991. He claims all his travel back home is "political," so he gets his campaign contributors to pay for his meals, newspapers, dry cleaning, and clothes.[1]

Using all these perks wouldn't be possible without careful organization and planning, much of it coordinated by a little-known group of twenty-three men and one woman who call themselves the House Administration Committee of the U.S. Congress. They oversee the three facets of congressional life that are reflected in everything else—elections, staff, and perquisites.

If the Appropriation Committee is solemnly called the College of Cardinals, the House Administration Committee must be the Graduate School of Greed. Its daily deliberations determine who gets the money for special junkets, how much can be spent on lavish office decorations, where the latest computers go, how much muscle goes into enforcing election laws, and where the funds for subsidizing meals, medicine, stationery, shoeshines, haircuts, handball courts, cars, and campaign staff are hidden. The power of this Favor Factory is in the privileges it provides to members—Members Only.

The first requirement of privilege, of course, is recognition—and Congress spares no expense in ensuring that even the most reticent representative is recognizable. What other line of work lavishes its executives with round-the-clock photographers, personal press agents, radio and television studios, and endless mountains of embossed propaganda? The "star system" may be dead in Hollywood, but it's flourishing in the hallowed halls of Congress.

The creation of public recognition serves two important purposes. First, it is the foundation of all incumbency-protection strategies. Ask the average voter why his vote went to an incumbent whose voting record he despises and you will inevitably hear: "I never see his opponent. The incumbent is always 'here,' I see him on TV, he writes me often, he's always in the papers." The congressional propaganda machine creates a constant, recognizable presence that ensures reelection. And, with modern technology, most of it can be done without going "home" to the district.

Secondly, recognition greases the palm of privilege. For most incumbents, their face, their name, or if all else fails, their title (the Honorable), is all it takes to rake in the rewards. First-class air travel, for example, is free for the asking. Walk into a theater, club, or stadium—no ticket required. Recognition permits gracious decorum to hide the outrage of unbridled graft. Therefore, the picture, the profile, the persona must be everywhere—a task, in fact the only task, that Congress has mastered.

The House Administration Committee understands its role in this process: provide the members with whatever they need—whatever the cost, whatever the justification—to ensure that they are recognized, revered, respected, and reelected. From the mundane to the sublime, nothing is overlooked. Pictures, flags, souvenirs, maps, calendars, beepers, autopens, agricultural yearbooks, potted plants, radio actualities, television tapes, books, magazine articles, free research, debate coaches, even framed copies of speeches that were never spoken—these are the common currency of their craft. And don't forget the polished Lincolns with phones front and back, the helicopter rides to the nearest military base, and the state-of-the-art computers that "personalize" a thousand letters an hour—the inventory of congressional communication and recognition devices is never-ending, limited by no budget, no authority, no standard, no measure of morality. It goes on forever.

If any House member still isn't satisfied with the number of perks accorded him there is a court of final appeal: the Speaker. At the end of the year any money not spent by members on office expenses isn't returned to the Treasury. It is poured into something called the Speaker's discretionary fund, which as of February 1992 contained $46 million. The Speaker is free to spend this slush fund without worrying about audits or oversight hearings. "Any member can go to the Speaker and request a special appropriation for something he doesn't think he could otherwise get," notes former Rep. Bill Frenzel, now a scholar at the Brookings Institution.[2] Recently, the House leadership took $1.5 million from the slush fund and bought new bar code readers for the mail room to make it even easier for members to bombard their districts with propaganda. When the Democratic Steering and Policy Committee wanted to renovate a room for its meetings, the Speaker quietly allocated $314,000 from his discretionary fund for its use.

The second requirement for effective political privilege is uncontested control of the public purse. Earlier generations of unelected royalty simply stole from the public treasury to pay for everything from castles to concubines, enforcing their larceny with mercenary might. Today's modern member is more subtle. Although direct charges to the Treasury (of $3 billion or so) provide a generous salary, opulent surroundings, and a lifestyle that most kings would envy, the privileges that really count come obliquely through a process of legalized extortion.

The calculus of this corruption is simple. Congress controls nearly $2 trillion in spending and loan guarantees, not counting the half trillion in private spending mandated by its regulations or the litigation they produce. Every one of those dollars has a company, union, association, professional society, law firm, governmental body, school, or interest group fighting over it. If each of these "special interests" is willing to invest just one dollar for the privilege of making or saving $1,000, then Congress gets $2 billion to finance its fun. In the spirit of fairness and sharing, Congress carefully allocates the responsibility and authority over federal spending and regulation to scores of committees and subcommittees so that every member gets a piece of the pie. Without doubt, membership has its privileges, and "the privileged" have their members.

The last ingredient in this recipe for political privilege is time—the time to enjoy it all. Clearly, if members spent all their time legislating or campaigning, the joys of privilege would be wasted. The solution that has evolved over the past decades is simple, effective, and costly: hire staff to do the legislating and buy television time to do the campaigning. Total congressional staff, including shadow staffers like CRS and GAO researchers and analysts, has grown tenfold in forty years (to over 37,000). Spending on television has climbed fiftyfold in thirty years to over $150 million. As a result, members can enjoy the privileges that take time—the junkets to South America, the fishing trips to Alaska, the cruises, and the lavish receptions.

Of course, it's not enough just to be wined, dined, and entertained. His Incumbency deserves some "loot" as well. A golf outing in the summer of 1991 offers a good illustration of the impact of recent changes on the privileges of congressional life. Thirty years ago, few members of Congress played golf regularly in Washington. An occasional foursome could be found at Congressional Country Club, Burning Tree, or the Army-Navy Club. These days, in contrast, the "Annual Members Only Congressional Golf Tournament" breaks all records for attendance, caliber of golf, and, most of all, prizes. Held at the Andrews Air Force Base Golf Course (who else has its own Air Force Base with its own golf course?), it attracted over a hundred members on a warm Monday afternoon in June 1991. (Mondays and Fridays are *pro forma* days in Congress, i.e., days members get to enjoy their privileges.) With staff help from the Ways and Means Committee, the red carpet was rolled out. The private sector was expected to pitch in to do its bit.

The text of the invitation made it clear to every member that "each participant is expected to facilitate the Tournament's success by rounding-up district sponsors." "Sponsors" is a euphemism for extortees, the lobbyists, trade associations, utilities, banks, and law firms with money. They provided prizes—hundreds of prizes, thousands of prizes—each tagged with the donor's name (to meet disclosure rules).

When it was over, after eighteen holes of federal fairways and government greens, a hundred members, wined, dined, and even followed on the course by golf carts filled with beer, went up to get their prizes, conservatively estimated at over 2,500 prizes worth at least $75,000. There were twenty times more prizes than contestants! Every member walked away with two satchels full of prizes: shirts, golf clubs, cases of wine, radios, CD players, Virginia hams, Georgia peanut brittle, umbrellas, crystal, cameras, tools, and camping gear. Best of all, everyone was a winner! At first the emcee went through the protocol of announcing winners and letting them come up to receive their "prize," but soon it degenerated into a free-for-all as impatient members raided the prize tables. One member called the spectacle of members carrying off their booty "a feeding frenzy."

Incumbency has quite an appetite. Such gluttony is an acquired taste. You don't see too many freshmen members of Congress at these orgies of greed, unless they've had a similar diet of decadence in a state legislature or on some big city council. But it doesn't take long to learn to love such a lifestyle.

The golfing feeding frenzy took place on a day when, in other eras, Congress might have been crafting a balanced budget or overseeing the banking system. But in all fairness, the caliber of the golf that weekend was impressive. Several members broke par and admitted they played three or four times a week. With that kind of prizes-per-player ratio, it's not surprising.

But it's not fair to pick on just the golfers. Tennis, skiing, fishing, hunting, sailing, baseball, squash, or bridge, whatever the hobby or sport, not to mention the joys of the House gym, the members know how to play to win. These, however, are merely the sporting privileges, for a group of good sports. Consider, instead, some of the others—the joys of the game called Congress.

Let's start with the Clubhouse Privileges, the benefits that come with the territory of Capitol Hill. The story should start at the top, high above the Capitol Rotunda at the foot of the huge bronze statue of "Liberty," looking out across the incredible collection of marble and granite architecture that Congress calls home. Only members can escort you here, Washington's most private pinnacle, and show you the grandeur of their Clubhouse.

It is an incredible sight. Under the watchful eye of the House Administration Committee, the architect of the Capitol knows his job: surround members with opulence and privilege and spare no expense. Through miles of marble corridors, beneath thousands of dazzling chandeliers, among hundreds of cavernous chambers, walk the 535 House and Senate members who inhabit the world's most inefficient workplace, a temple of extravagance, ostentation, and wanton waste. The published records of construction and maintenance costs are only the tip of the iceberg. Conservative estimates of the annual occupancy costs for the average member's office exceed $400 per square foot, ten times the cost of deluxe downtown office space.

The newest congressional building, the Hart Senate Office Building, is, by far, the most expensive office building in Washington's history. But, as they say, the magic is in the details: The marble gym, with its weight rooms, massage tables, indoor pool, handball court—even a "dummy" office with desk, phone, and fake bookcase in case a photo of a busy member is suddenly required. . . The private subways, so you won't have to burn any of the fat cells you're saving for a workout in the gym. . . Scores of private elevators, staffed with what must be the only surviving members of the American Union of Elevator Operators, whose principal job is pointing out the "Members Only" sign to the tired taxpayers who foot the bill. . . The sunny South Balcony, shielded from public view, with its rows of elegant chaise lounges for midafternoon tan-maintenance therapy. . . The "hideaways," those cozy little offices public people need when their ordinary office suites are too public—after all, a member needs his space. . . The endless supply of artwork, statuary, and sculpture—national treasures loaned to brighten a member's day. . . The subsidized "everything"—cut-price meals, haircuts, carwashes, shoeshines, souvenirs, even a hidden gas tank where members can fill up for free. . . The photography studio where bureaucratic Bachrachs develop ten thousand glossies a day—each with a singularly sincere smile—and add that personal touch we all love, "To my dear friend," above the autograph of the AutoPen. . . The glorious Caucus and Committee rooms, temples to the egotism of powerful Speakers and chairmen, who measure their magnificence by the height of the ceiling, the width of the chandelier, and the gallons of gilt. . . .

Even the collateral buildings of Congress have taken on the trappings of majesty. The Library of Congress, Congressional Research Service, House Information System, and, yes, Police Headquarters, occupy lavish new or refurbished quarters, although the mighty members themselves hardly ever stop by. But when privilege is translated into bricks and mortar, marble and gilt, mahogany and silk, it's always done in the name of "the people." Modest members forswear any personal interest in a lavish Capitol. It is, after all, a public treasure—and the public deserves the best, the biggest, the most expensive. America can afford it and deserves no less (and neither do they).

But from the top of the Capitol an astute observer can see another, more ironic symbol of political privilege. Not far away on an obscure corner of the Capitol's roof a group of workmen are continuously raising and lowering the American flag. Every minute a new flag is attached to the halyard, flown for a moment "over the Capitol," and carefully folded, boxed, and certificated, soon on its way to a naive constituent forever grateful to his member for sending him *the* flag that flew over the Capitol that day. A thousand flags a day will be transformed into personal symbols of a member's prestige. He alone can hand out these flags; it is his privilege to package patriotism. A cynic might say that it doesn't seem like quite a fair trade. Taxpayers get the flags that flew over the Capitol; members get the Capitol and everything else that isn't nailed down in Washington.

Envision, for example, the endless entertainment. Shows at the Kennedy Center, receptions in the Smithsonian, serenades by Army, Navy, and Air Force Bands, concerts on the Capitol Steps, recitals at the Library of Congress, and catered dinners in Statuary Hall, the National Archives, Union Station, or the National Art Gallery. And all of it free, subject only to the respective institution's continued funding by Congress.

But even with all this glitter, Washington can get boring, sometimes even distasteful, especially when the press starts complaining about how little esteem we all have for our Congress, wondering why the deficit's so big, or crying that the banks are going bust. Going "home" to the district offers little relief, so what's a member to do? Turn on the congressional travel machine, of course—the privilege most members rank as Number One.

Congressional travel is unique in several ways. First, travel arrangements and accommodations are exceptional. While corporate honchos brag about their private planes, consider that Congress has its own air force—helicopters, Gulfstreams, Learjets—not to mention thousands of vehicles and an army of chauffeurs. Helicopters pick them up a few discreet blocks away in Southeast Washington and government jets are waiting at Andrews Air Force Base, which even has its own expressway straight to the Capitol. Of course, every member has some kind of military facility near his district to serve his needs when he's "home."

But the temptations of congressional travel are even more alluring when the member arrives in a foreign country. Officially known as a CoDel (Congressional Delegation), the bane of any ambassador's life, a group of junketing members behaves and expects to be treated like the offspring of a marriage between Donald Trump and Zsa Zsa Gabor. Chauffeured to every tourist sight, feted at sumptuous private dinners, and completely exempt from the normal burdens of travel, like custom duties, immigration inspections, or airport queues, they view foreign travel as their most cherished privilege, their right to flight.

The perquisites don't even stop once a member ceases being a member. Congress has one of the most generous retirement systems ever conceived, and a member qualifies after only six years in office. Many members collect well over a million dollars after retirement from their monthly pension checks alone.

Former House Speaker Tip O'Neill collects $6,250 every month from his congressional retirement. Former Sen. Richard Schweiker of Pennsylvania will have collected a total of $1,743 million in pension checks if he lives to the 83.2 years actuaries project.[3] Schweiker's salary when he retired in 1980 after eighteen years in Congress was $60,663 a year.

These cushy congressional pensions are padded by something called "the kicker," a cost-of-living adjustment that boosts their pensions faster than the rate of inflation. In the cloakrooms of Congress, these add-ons are called "cost-of-luxury adjustments." Hastings Keith, a former congressman from Massachusetts who left office in 1972, gives a first-hand account of how "the kicker" works: when he retired at age fifty-seven, his pension from six years in the military, fourteen years in Congress, and three months in the Civil Service was $1,560 a month. Today it is a whopping $5,506 a month. So far, Hastings Keith has received over $1 million in federal pensions, nearly half due to "the kicker."[4]

While members are still in office, they enjoy yet another privilege, the true jewel in their crown, a privilege unique to them, a privilege that shields them from all the petty slings and arrows of mortal life and places them securely on a pedestal above all other Americans—the privilege to write their own rules.

We live in a world of rules and regulations that dictate what we can say, where we can go, to whom we must bow and scrape. Congress is, in short, exempt. Exempt from the rules *it* passes for the rest of us that circumscribe our life, our workplace, our bank account, our freedoms, rights, and responsibilities. But most of all, they exempt themselves from the ethical standards of our times.

Those who make the law thumb their nose at it. From the trivial, like traffic and parking violations, to the profound, like the violations of other human beings, lawmakers live in a world whose standards are different, subject only to what they think they can't hide. A never-ending story unfolds mindlessly in our modern media, filled with names like Hart, Lukens, Kennedy, Bauman, Cranston, Frank, Jenrette, and hundreds more whose transgressions are only known within the Clubhouse.

Not only do they make their own rules, they can almost guarantee that anyone who breaks them goes unpunished. Consider the name of their internal court of highest review, the Select Committee on Ethics. Does it function to "select" which rules to ignore, to "select" which members to shield, to "select" which evidence to hide? Their own counsel in the recent Keating Five hearings could only cringe at their gutless behavior. Everyone was guilty, so the Select Committee on Ethics said, "Let them all go free."

The privilege to make your own rules is the crucial privilege—it's the insurance policy for all the others. In its most venal form it works to rig the rules of our nation's elections, crafting a Members Only version of modern election law that has emasculated the contests so critical to effective democracy. Incumbents have made themselves unbeatable by abusing the assets of their office, hiring an army of reelection campaigners at taxpayer expense, extorting funds to brainwash the electorate with execrable campaign commercials, and creating what antitrust lawyers call barriers to entry in the form of procedural hurdles that intimidate all but the most durable opponents.

But now the ones without privileges call for reform—the rest of America that watches the party from outside the castle, standing in the rain of rising taxes, hearing the thunder of impending economic collapse, and afraid of the darkening portent of an America in decline. They ask themselves how to get control, how to get the powerful to listen, how to create a system where the privileges of this new class of political professionals can be checked. Today the officeholders view part of their jobs as throwing up enough political static so the voters can't come up with the answers. If they succeed, the membership can retain all its privileges.

# 3

# DO WE HAVE ELECTIONS ANYMORE?

*The House of Representatives is becoming too impenetrable to be representative.*

—DAVID MAYHEW,
professor of government at Yale University.


A VISIT TO colonial Williamsburg reminds how far we've come in building and refining our concept of an effective and democratic legislature, and how some other things haven't changed. The local print shop sells caricatures of politicians, circa 1762, and some of the roving troubadours sing ditties that ridicule lawyers and political windbags. But during the more serious historical discussions, the guides are quick to point out the democratic shortcomings of the colonial legislature that sat in Williamsburg 250 years ago.

If you take the tour of the reconstructed colonial capitol, you can sit in the seats of the House of Burgesses, the lower house of Virginia's prerevolutionary legislature. The guide strides around the room, stopping at the historic Speaker's chair with its distinctive high back so evocative of the British Parliament, and asks the assembled tourists to imagine they are citizens of colonial Virginia and potential members of that historic legislative body.

He asks you all to stand as he begins a simple demonstration of colonial political power. The House of Burgesses, he says, is venerated today as the historic precursor of our modern legislatures; but how does it really compare?

"Each of you," he explains, "represents a typical Virginian of the period, but how many of you could be members of this legislature? First, those of you who are slaves or indentured servants please sit down, because you aren't welcome here."

One man takes his seat with the remark, "I guess that means me, since I work for the government." The rest salute his wit with some anxious laughter.

"Now," says your guide, "will everyone under twenty-one take a seat." A dozen youngsters, a few college students, and several enlisted men from a nearby boot camp sit down.

"The ladies are next. All of you. This was strictly a single-sex legislature." By this point, only a third of the room is still standing.

The polite colonial Williamsburg guide now discretely advises that anyone without great wealth or property should remove himself from the running. You need a minimum of twenty-five acres of land to be a burgess.

By this point, only one unhumbled man is still on his feet. "Are you, by any chance, an Anglican?" asks your host. The somewhat chagrined Presbyterian takes his seat.

"So none of you could become members of this august legislative body. Not quite the democracy you thought, is it?" he concludes.

If our modern Congress were to give its visitors the same lesson in democracy, the inquisition would be over much faster. No inquiries needed about servitude, sex, age, religion, or even affluence. The only question: "Are you an incumbent?"

Your chances as a challenger today are not much better than a ten-year-old agnostic female landless slave in Williamsburg.

One wonders if Patrick Henry, Thomas Jefferson, or James Madison could win a congressional seat this year—or would even try.

The wonderful political ideas and debates that echoed across colonial America from the Kings Arms Inn in Williamsburg to City Tavern in Philadelphia were all about creating a government that would be subservient to the people and yet be able to resist the recognized evils of tyranny and bureaucracy. The people's first line of defense was to be the Congress.

Creating Congress was the most important part of creating a new government. It was clearly the branch of government closest to the people, and therefore needed the power to assert their authority, but debate raged as to what mechanisms would prevent its members from being seduced by the very powers they had been granted.

Their legislative output was made subject to presidential veto and judicial review, and, of course, the will of each body of Congress was to be carefully constrained by the other. But the principal means of preventing legislative tyranny was, by design, the congressional election.

 The Senate was to be chosen by state legislatures, whose members' individual ambitions were seen as an effective check on senatorial arrogance and abuse. Senators would doubtless be individuals of experience who reflected the political positions of the legislative majority back home.

House elections were cautiously scheduled every two years so that no member was far removed from popular review or recall. Our Founding Fathers had several decades of experience observing colonial legislatures like the House of Burgesses, and were familiar with the sins of the politically powerful. They had seen neighbors head off to their colony's capital full of resolve to oppose a current policy, only to see them return as defenders of government actions they had once criticized.

Even more worrisome, they had seen ordinary citizens enter

public office and quickly assume the trappings of royalty. They therefore insisted on frequent elections to force those who had been seduced by power to give it up. America's congressional elections would thus expose tyrants before they became entrenched.

With the help of Providence and not a little luck, Congress survived for well over a century with this competitive format intact. At the time of Alexis de Tocqueville's visit to America in 1832, congressional politics was the leading national pastime, and every two years brought lively debate, new candidates, and the kind of excitement that citizens today seem to find only in the World Series or the Superbowl.

Each Congress throughout the nineteenth century was a substantially different political entity. Usually, 40 to 60 percent of each Congress was composed of new members, and new alliances, new leaders, and new ideas allowed government to respond quickly to the needs of a rapidly growing and changing country. The status quo, along with existing seniority and orthodoxy, was thrown out at the end of every even-numbered year. The following year brought renewed energy and enthusiasm—and fresh faces from top to bottom. In 1811, for example, Henry Clay was elected to his first term in Congress and elected Speaker his first day on the job! Back then, of course, the work of congressmen was much more difficult. Traveling to Washington was back-breaking, literally, and once there, the lifestyle was hardly luxurious. Congressmen wrote their own letters and speeches, did their own research, undertook their own investigations and oversight, and even managed their own elections. Perhaps few people wanted the job once they discovered the demands and working conditions, or maybe the public was just harder to please in those days; in any case, the average congressman didn't keep his job very long.

In 1852, for example, only 36.2 percent of the members of the House of Representatives had served there previously, the average congressman having a tenure of just seventeen months in Congress. In 1894, the situation was not much different: half the House members were freshmen. As the twentieth century began, material conditions started to improve in Washington. Opulent congressional office buildings were constructed and national affluence, coupled with the legalization of the income tax, provided government with vast new financial resources. As the nation discovered the limits of its Western frontier, its government discovered that it could grow up, as well as out. Congress led the way.

The life of a congressman also began to improve. Transportation improvements made journeys to Washington far more pleasant, and the development of the capital city, as trolley lines pushed west and north, opened up opportunities for real estate speculation and other profitable "investments" by well-connected solons. The city itself blossomed, as swamps were drained, streets paved, and scores of plush new hotels and restaurants opened. Washington had finally become a real city with all the comforts of home, and serving in Congress became something more as well: Now it could be a career.

The year 1900 was the first in which incoming members of Congress averaged more than four years of prior "experience," and never again would a new Congress have less. By 1908, for the first time, more than 90 percent of Congress would seek reelection, and in 1916 less than 20 percent of the House was made up of newcomers, a record low at the time. Congress was becoming an institution, and membership was becoming institutionalized. By 1929, the average member had served more than eight years in Congress.

In the 1960s Congress unleashed the Great Society on America, and it made incredible improvements in its own standard of living at the same time. Lavish new office buildings were constructed to house career congressmen and their enlarged staffs, which had doubled in size in less than a decade. Computers, Xerox machines, and the wonders of the television age multiplied the reality of congressional existence a thousandfold. Even more ominously, the canyons of the K Street corridor in "downtown" D.C. began to fill with legions of lobbyists and trade associations that promised each congressman an affluent retirement. Congress had become the career of choice.

More than 91 percent of Congress sought reelection throughout the 1960s, and in 1969, for the first time in history, over 90 percent of the members taking the oath of office had taken it before. Still, the Age of the Imperial Congress had only begun.

As late as 1980 it was still possible for challengers to mount vigorous campaigns, because political action committees still had the courage to support insurgent candidates. But in the mid-1980s that all changed, when at the direction of the House leadership, major PACs were told that donations to challengers would be *remembered* if they ever wanted any congressional favors. PAC donations to challengers evaporated overnight, falling from 50 percent of total PAC contributions in 1980 to less than 5 percent in 1990. The result was the final nail in the coffin of competitive congressional elections. Career politicians had won!

In the four congressional elections from 1984 to 1990, the incumbents were king. No similar span in American history can match the total dominance by incumbents in the House of Representatives: 97 percent of all incumbents were reelected. In 1988, the figure was an unbelievable 98.3 percent! Today, the average representative has "served" twelve years in Congress, an all-time high.

During those 4 elections, only 43 members were defeated in the general election (16 in 1984, 6 in 1986, 6 in 1988, and 15 in 1990). A century ago (1890-96), 237 incumbents were defeated over 8 years, and this at a time when Congress was 20 percent smaller.[1]

All this is not to say that Congress does not change from year to year. It does, but the changes reflect mutations in the incumbents themselves or decisions about leaving that *they* make, not the voter.

Incumbents, it must be understood, undergo a magical metamorphosis as they "progress" through their congressional careers. Like a mosquito, their political life involves complete transformations from one stage to another—from egg to larva, pupa, and finally, adult.

The egg stage represents their precongressional life and profession, if any. For most modern career politicians, this formative period began when they were elected hallway monitor in the fourth grade.

When the teacher let them skip a long division review session to attend a "meeting" of all the hallway monitors, they learned the meaning of privilege. When they issued their first warning to a tardy third-grader, they came to appreciate the possibilities of power. And when they saw they could make friends by bending the rules, they understood the meaning of pork.

The egg stage progresses through high school and college and, in most cases, law school. Good grades aren't as important as collecting extracurricular contacts or winning an internship with an aging politician. With luck, they can avoid any real work (except cramming to pass the bar exams), advancing directly to a staff job in a member's office or the state capital, or even election to the state legislature.

Some of these congressional eggs have more traditional backgrounds in business, journalism, education, or the law, but most are nurtured somewhere on the fringes of politics: university political science departments, school boards, lobbying operations, PR firms, trade associations, unions, or environmental groups. Early on, they decide to pursue a "career" in Congress, driven more by ambition than idealism, by opportunism than principle.

If they can pick the right open seat in the right state in the right year and campaign on the right issue with friends in the right places, they can win. Otherwise, they wait until the right time comes. Like mosquito eggs in a stagnant pond, they'll wait for the rainy season. When it comes, they're elected and the metamorphosis begins.

The freshman congressman is an entirely new animal (or insect?) that has abandoned most of the trappings of his or her previous incarnation as political campaigner. No longer do you hear: "And I promise that if elected I will. . . . " Now, it's: "The congressman is busy now, but he does have a fundraiser scheduled and maybe. . . ."

It seems that this larval stage produces an organism with a tremendous appetite for publicity, flattery, and campaign donations, as we will explore more fully in later chapters. The career congressman knows that this is the most critical stage of his political development. Now is the time to build a layer of insulating cash, perhaps as much as a million dollars, to protect him from potential enemies as his metamorphosis continues.

The freshman congressman is undefined, malleable, subject to persuasion and temptation, and, along with everyone else in this sordid swamp along the Potomac, he understands this truism: Now is when he can be bought. He has debts to retire and a war chest to build. He is, at this stage, at his neediest.

Thus, it isn't surprising that many larval legislators now learn to live off the lobbyists, and vice versa. Constituents don't care or even know about this secret symbiosis, but it's fundamental to the career congressman's future development. By granting a few microscopic crumbs from the tax or appropriation bills to some well-heeled lobbyists, he can salt away enough to sustain his career through almost any political catastrophe.

It takes only a few terms of this to graduate to the next stage, the political pupa. Having become attached to Congress at this point, the typical member establishes his territory and defines his authority. Though not yet part of the elite, he works carefully to build his own base of power and influence. By this time, he has established himself as invincible in his district, and begun to assert control over some small corner of government through his committee assignments. At this stage, he worries less about reelection and more about perquisites. This is when he will start bouncing checks, sneaking funds out of the campaign account, and signing up for junkets to Barbados.

Before long, he's a full-fledged career congressman, for whom a decade or more of elections and logrolling have produced a kind of legislative inertia. Everything keeps grinding on—speeches drone on and on about the same national needs that must be met and how new programs are the answer. Every day is carefully choreographed by dozens of staffers who tell him where to go, what to say, and when to say it. But he can say it in his sleep. He never tires of being "shocked and dismayed" by runaway spending, unfair taxes, and bureaucratic waste. Most of all, he doesn't really care anymore.

He is, after all, unbeatable. No one can touch him, or even get close, since he's surrounded by 1,500 Capitol police— more than the entire force of Baltimore, Maryland—who keep the common folks at bay. He's built a career that will be in the history books someday—part of the modern empire we call Congress.

Someday, it comes to an end. The career in Congress is over—the mosquito has feasted, sucked its victim dry, and is ready to reproduce a whole new generation of electoral insects. Whatever the terminology, even in this era of imperial careers, this is when we get some turnover in Congress. In fact, term limitation opponents always point out how much "turnover" we have.

These opponents, it seems, confuse the turnover caused by voters with the turnover caused by the incumbents themselves. Let's look, then, at the real reasons members of Congress have left office over the past four elections.

There are six fundamental determinants of congressional "turnover":

1. Members voluntarily retire or resign. This is especially significant in 1992 because senior members can transfer surplus campaign funds to their personal account only if they retire by the end of 1992. Like the opposite of a signing bonus for a baseball superstar, these retiring members get a huge bonus if they head for the showers now. Over sixty members of the House and Senate are retiring this year: at least a third of these reflect the influence of the "retirement bonus."

2. They run for or accept appointment to higher office. This is especially attractive for House members this year, many of whom find themselves victimized by the gerrymandering of their old districts. Fourteen members are taking this way out in 1992—eleven Senate-hopefuls, two aspiring governors, and one new cabinet member.

3. They die. Only two, so far, in the current Congress, but usually three or four per cycle.

4. They are victims of reapportionment or gerrymandering. Sometimes their districts disappear in the once-a-decade remapping that shifts dozens of seats from one part of the country to another. More typically, they suffer from the partisan redrawing of districts that can send half their constituents to a different district or surgically remove just enough precincts to give the other party control on election day. This accounts for as many as thirty or forty turnovers each decade.

5. They are arrested, indicted, or tainted with credible allegations of corruption or scandal. Abscam, Wedtech, Donna Rice, Charles Keating, and the House Bank are all memorials to this fast-growing type of turnover. Catch a congressman on tape doing something criminal and he's no longer unbeatable, though it may take a few years to

send him packing. Rep. Austin Murphy was repri-
manded by the House in 1987 for letting other members
cast votes for him and for keeping a ghost employee on
his payroll, but he has managed to hang on, even though
he won his 1992 primary with just 36 percent of the vote.

Scandal-based campaigning is the new political reality;
the only way incumbents can be brought back to earth, it
seems, is if they bring themselves down into the mud. Of
the six incumbents defeated in 1988, five were facing
some criminal or ethical indictment. This year's House
Bank scandal may lead to the defeat of as many as thirty
members, but in a normal year usually no more than four
or five fall because of such malfeasance in office.

6. And the sixth reason? The least likely reason for a person
to leave Congress is by being defeated in an open, non-
reapportioned, competitive election, free from hints of
corruption or scandal. No more than twenty members of
the House or Senate have suffered such an indignity over
the past decade.[2]

Maybe that's why, for most of us, elections are such a joke.
The Founding Fathers hoped to check would-be congressional
tyrants, but now we look at them as little more than the political equivalent of microwave popcorn. Throw some corn, some
salt, and a bit of grease into this electoral oven (you don't even
have to take it out of the packaging), blast it with electronic
radiation in thirty-second doses (TV commercials) until the
popping stops, and presto—it's done. You've got another Congress that looks and smells pretty much like the last one, with
only a few dead kernels in the bottom of the bag.

The last congressional election in Virginia is a good example. Suppose Thomas Jefferson, James Madison, or Patrick
Henry had come back to see how their safeguard against
tyranny—the election—was working. They'd have found
John Warner, the Republican incumbent, running for the

Senate. But he had no Democratic opponent! He nevertheless spent $1,152,000 getting reelected. Not much competition there.

At the same time, five incumbent Democrats were running for reelection to the House. Here, too, not one had a Republican opponent! But all together, they spent $1,128,000 in their campaigns. You wonder how both parties could be so uncompetitive in the same state until you realize that party affiliations are increasingly meaningless to incumbents. Incumbency is their real party. Staying in office is their only platform.

Not surprisingly, the voters and media are resentful. They're worried about their government and upset with Congress—only 17 percent, an all-time low, approve of the job that Congress is doing. The same poll shows that 73 percent of all Americans feel "the entire political system is broken. It's run by insiders who don't listen to working people and are incapable of solving our problems." A full 60 percent (61 percent Republicans and Independents, 59 percent Democrats) agree with the statement: "Congress never seems to get anything done, so maybe we ought to replace them all, including my congressman."[3]

Millions of Americans, regrettably, are turned off. "Elections are rigged, so why bother," they say. According to *Congressional Quarterly*'s Rhodes Cook, if you factor out districts where there's a contest for governor or senator to lure people, the turnout for congressional elections (the percentage of people over eighteen who actually vote) is only 27.6 percent.[4]

But can you really blame them? In 20 percent of all House races, the incumbent had no major party opponent in the previous election. Most of the rest are almost as one-sided. Common Cause estimates that incumbents have so much money and so many advantages that only 10 percent of all House contests are truly competitive. The rest are foregone conclusions.[5] Rep. David Dreier compares the way incumbents neutralize competition with the way some authoritarian countries run their elections. "What we in Congress do is in a small way similar to how Danny Ortega tried to fix elections in Nicaragua," he says.[6]

Still, it must be remembered that miracles can happen. Daniel Ortega lost his elections, and this year in America some observers see signs that the logjam of incumbency may be loosening for this one year. The House Bank Scandal is broader and more far reaching than any such scandal since the Credit Mobilier railroad scandal of 1873 that turned more than 42 percent of House incumbents out of office in the next election. Recent polls show that public disapproval of Congress is at record levels, and that, for the first time, voters are prepared to vote against their *own* congressman.

Many incumbents are worried, but most seem confident they can ride out the storm and stonewall efforts at meaningful reform, including calls for term limits.

A senior member, sitting in the back row of Congress late one night this spring as the House was voting to release the names of overdrafters in the House Bank Scandal, gave this cynical assessment of the political fortunes of his colleagues this year: "Sure, we're going to lose a few members because of all these bad checks, maybe a dozen or two, but it won't be that bad for most of us. We'll survive. And after it's all over we can relax, because if we can survive this one, we'll know that *nothing* can knock us out."

The sad thing is that, with all the advantages incumbents have, he may just be right.

# 4

## THE ART OF INCUMBENCY

IT'S A WONDERFUL CAREER, being a congressman. Every day offers new rewards: new wrongs to right, new dreams to dream, new frontiers to cross.

But at the end of the day most members are left with the painful realization that this idealized life of accomplishment is a fraud—a monument to deceit and deception where little of value is produced, and where reputation comes from the manipulation of public opinion by an army of sycophantic staff and all the other high-tech weapons in the arsenal of Incumbency.

A sinister symbiosis evolves between the member and his handlers, those staffers who fabricate and then feed on his career as a congressman. An unspoken contract is drawn among these various opportunists: The congressman is allowed to be called "Congressman" and "the Honorable," to be introduced by pompous political windbags as "a great leader," to be pampered by the press and pandered to by lobbyists. In return, many a member allows his handlers to write his speeches, author his bills, shape his policies, and get him reelected.

The only real work expected of many a member is the daily drudgery known as "dialing for dollars"—raising campaign cash—and a willingness to turn himself on whenever a voter or television camera comes near. He doesn't have to follow up on anything, not even on the promises he makes. He is merely the front man—or rather, the surface transparency.

His artful handlers fill in this political picture with promises, press releases, patronage, and pounds and pounds of paper. They tell him how to color his beliefs and when to shade his rhetoric with innuendo or prejudice. They direct the spotlight of public attention on his carefully sculpted initiatives and shield his indiscretions behind dark clouds of distortion or smokescreens of silence. At reelection time, many take a "leave of absence" and work on the campaign directly. In 1990, over 40 percent of congressmen running for reelection installed a personal aide in a top job on their campaigns.[1]

Through assiduous work, congressional staffers shape a member's political future by creating a flattering portrait of the congressman. Reproduced a million times through the wonders of modern PR technology, he soon becomes a public commodity, a bankable political asset. He becomes *His Incumbency*.

This modern Machievelli is, as always, a product of privilege. Incumbency confers on him a dowry of political advantage undreamed of by history's most ambitious schemers. It provides scores of special benefits both obvious and subtle, harmless and destructive, trivial and decisive. It surrounds him with a cachet of accomplishment and the appearance of power. But, in truth, it is the most bankrupt of all political strategies: to win reelection by abusing the privileges of the office and spending the taxpayers' own money to buy their vote.

Reelection strategy begins the day after election, even before he's officially sworn in. Almost instantly, he can feed at the public trough, and it doesn't take long to develop an appetite for spending other people's money.

It's two months from election day to the start of a new Congress. The official paychecks won't start until he has sworn to uphold the Constitution, etc., and voted for the new

Speaker, but by then he's had nine weeks of free phones, free mail, free public relations, free computers, and the freedom that comes with calling yourself the incumbent. And already he's begun to think about the next election and to use his office to ensure his reelection.

Someone once said (it was probably a politician) that "knowledge is power." Today's incumbent congressman has distilled the truth of this saying to three principles that are his political essence:

Know my name. Know my face. Know my power.

The purpose of the incumbency machine is to distribute this "knowledge" to his constituents, and almost every element of the institution called Congress has been designed to further this objective.

From his first days as congressman-elect, he is taught how to use incumbency to advance these three central objectives. His party's congressional committee indoctrinates him within weeks in the wonders of computerized "casework," radio and television "actualities," targeted direct mail, franked "postal patron mailings," and time-tested techniques to get his name in the papers.

His staff structure is professionally prescribed for him: twenty-two full-time employees in the House, distributed among his Washington and up-to-eight district offices, all of whom know their only job is to win the next election.

Five or six concentrate on casework and constituent service, euphemisms for creating a cadre of political debtors. Three or four more are "correspondence managers," masters of the computerized direct mail operation that can send out thousands of personalized letters every day. Another pair usually woo the media full time, while someone else takes on the role of surrogate public speaker, playing congressman before Rotaries, high schools, and garden clubs.

Add to these someone to answer the phone cheerfully (always put the emphasis on the word *congressman*) and to place his calls (especially when he's looking for money), someone to drive him to his appointments (and brief him on who'll be there, how many votes they have, and where the money is), and someone to schedule his time (and make sure that everyone who sees him contributes to his reelection).

That leaves two or three senior aides to plot his reelection strategy, decide which bills to introduce or cosponsor, author the speeches he delivers (or at least has inserted into the *Congressional Record*), choose which committee meetings to attend, and define which positions, if any, to stake out in the interest of the voters back home.

One of these, the legislative assistant, toils to create scores of superficial legislative proposals to "throw in the hopper"(now, there's a fitting metaphor if ever there was one): bills to create parks, roads, bridges, hospitals, schools, wilderness areas, scenic rivers, research centers, and demonstration programs that everyone in Washington knows will never become reality. But reality isn't important to an incumbent. His art is modern—impressionistic, abstract, distorted, even absurd.

When interviewing for these positions, dozens of ambitious young men and women declare their undying allegiance to the member, his district and state, and his political positions. Most of them, of course, have few, if any, political values or beliefs; and if they do, they'll happily sacrifice them all for the chance to work for an incumbent. They understand the unwritten contract: get *him* reelected and enjoy *their* power.

The contract also stipulates that the taxpayers underwrite all this. It is the most important point of reality for His Incumbency. He doesn't have to pay for anything—all these people working for his reelection are free, and so is everything else. Thus it is written.

But that's not the only thing that gets written. His staffers soon learn that their real output is The Word. Every idea has to be translated into a press release, every day is designed to seduce assignment editors to cover His Incumbency, and every event or issue is a chance to spread The Word. The most important word is His Name.

It is no exaggeration to say that His Incumbency will cause His Name to be printed or listened to on radio or seen on television more than a billion times in a typical congressional term. The simple goal of an incumbent's media operation is to have every one of his constituents read or hear his name at least three times a week. Many say they don't even care if the "press hit" is favorable, as long as the name is spelled right.

The printing presses of power politics are truly prodigious. An average incumbent will send out a few million pieces of franked mail each year. Less than one-tenth of 1 percent goes out in response to letters or phone calls from constituents. The most ubiquitous franked mail pieces are the newsletters, those four- to eight-page journals of self-promotion, complete with testimonials from fellow incumbents, pictures with celebrities, and reprints of any favorable editorials from back home. Long criticized as outrageous examples of taxpayer-financed propaganda, they are still being published at record levels. Sometimes the uses to which franked mail is put is enough to make the blood boil. After Sen. Al D'Amato, a New York Republican, was only given a mild rebuke by the Senate Ethics Committee for allowing influence-peddling activities in his office, he had the gall to send a taxpayer-financed letter to every household in his state claiming he had been exonerated.

A few years back, in an effort to placate growing public anger at these flagrant abuses of the franking privilege, Congress passed some "rules" limiting the form and use of these franked newsletters. One restriction limits the number of times the member's name can be included on each page (no more than eight times per page). Another states that franked mail cannot be delivered to the House and Senate Post Offices within sixty days of an election, though the backlog of franked mail dumped on them just before an election is such that much of it goes out after the deadline. In 1990, two hundred employees in the House folding room were working seventy-hour weeks without overtime to get out mailings that helped incumbents in their primaries.

Rep. Chris Cox of California says the reforms that have been passed to reform franked mail are "wholly cosmetic."[2] Certainly, Congress continues to have big plans for franked mail. There is talk of building a giant new congressional mailing office on twenty-five acres of federal land in Maryland.[3]

More magical, perhaps, than the newsletters and the other districtwide mailings (e.g., Town Meeting notices, voting record summaries, announcements of such things as 800-numbers and new office locations and voter registration reminders), which are designed almost exclusively to broaden name recognition, are the modern computer mailing systems.

A modern incumbent views his constituents as one huge database. His goal is to get every voter's name, address, and political profile into his computer's memory.

During his first days in office, he seduces his constituents with questionnaires and surveys, hoping to solicit responses that will allow him to categorize each voter into one of hundreds of ideological groups, from prolife to anti-death penalty.

Environmentalists, Zionists, senior citizens (broken down by birth year so different subgroups like "notch-babies" can be targeted), parochial school parents, union families, gun owners, farmers, and members of various fraternal organizations are typical categories. Newly registered voters, high school and college graduates, new parents, and new house buyers receive friendly letters of welcome and congratulations, urging them to fill out a questionnaire and "write about issues of concern."

Before long, an incumbent has a detailed file on almost every likely voter, supplemented by computerized data he buys to cross-tabulate income level, precinct, voting history, and educational background. He can tell who is likely to be interested in proposals to balance the budget or expand tuition tax credits, who will appreciate his vote for the economic reform package or his vote *against* the veto override of the same bill, and who will want a new agricultural planting calendar or copies of his speech praising the local high school band.

The key to the computer operation is the sophisticated correspondence management software provided to each member's office by private consultants or by the Congress's own House Information System, a mammoth multimillion dollar computer empire that can bring the latest computer technology to well-connected incumbents.

Every day, a new "targeted mailing" is designed, produced, and mailed, all at taxpayers' expense, of course. The mailings range from a few dozen letters to several thousand, each artfully composed and personalized to hide any hint of mass production. The autopen provides a facsimile of the member's signature, and many even add preprinted or computerized hand-written postscripts like "I thought you'd be interested in this—See you soon!"

The effect is incredible. Voters otherwise sophisticated and skeptical are naively impressed that His Incumbency took the time to write such a personal note. They are, furthermore, usually enticed to respond, and so begins the process that transforms the voter into a friend.

This means that his name is upgraded on the computer database. He graduates from someone in an "issue" file to someone in one of the many "friend of member" files. Soon, he will be entitled to birthday greetings, Christmas cards, special invitations to fundraisers, and inclusion in the "Inner Circle." All this can be done entirely within the computer "fulfillment" operation, without so much as a vague awareness of the special relationship by His Incumbency himself.

Chicanery like this often risks exposure, as when a frequent correspondent, convinced that he receives frequent *personal* letters from His Incumbency, actually meets the member at an unexpected venue. But most incumbents handle such surprises smoothly—they are, after all, common occurrences during visits back to the district.

"I really appreciated your letter yesterday," says the grateful constituent. The congressman quickly scans his face looking for clues about the subject in question. Calmly, he responds, "I had been thinking of writing to you for several days and took the time to dictate it after I got home late one night."

By then, the smiling constituent is an official "friend." His Incumbency pumps his hand forcefully, pats his back, gives him his "sincere look"(two seconds of eye contact), and smoothly effects an escape. A moment later, he'll ask his "name-keeper" aide for a positive ID, so that if the constituent reappears he can loudly salute his good friend, John Doe.

A first-class correspondence management system will successfully prospect and categorize at least 40 percent of the registered voters in a typical congressional district. Each of these fortunate constituents will receive four or more personalized letters each year, and, with luck, as many as thirty thousand can be upgraded to "friends."

A few months later, these "friends" are quietly turned over to the campaign database. There they may become potential donors and campaign volunteers. In any event, a few nights before the election they get a "personal" phone call from His Incumbency's phone bank to remind them to vote. In almost every case, these "friends" can guarantee reelection.

There are a score of other "friendship-building" strategies that most members exploit using other incumbency benefits. These range from the mundane, like the flags "flown over the Capitol," framed certificates, or even citations in the *Congressional Record*, to the sublime, like Superbowl tickets (donated by lobbyists) or invitations to special political events sponsored by every member (cocktails with the president or Speaker of the House during a campaign swing through his district).

Other friendships are cemented with more procedural association with His Incumbency. Most members, for example, will create scores and scores of "official" task forces, councils, advisory boards, and selection committees. These give their professional friends evidence of their special relationship with the Honorable and demonstrate his power at the same time. The taxpayers provide staff to do the "official" work, if any, required by the various groups, but the friends get the prestige and, in most cases, understand the unwritten campaign contribution quid pro quo.

But politicians have always known they had to "influence people" as well as "win friends"—an early recognition, perhaps, of the fact that "friends" alone can't win elections anymore. Friends can be fickle and unreliable. Often, they take the outcome for granted, or forget to cast their ballot on election day.

Nonfriends, in any case, are the problem. They don't have that close personal relationship that "friends" have with His Incumbency. Besides, America has become so mobile that half his friends will move away in a few years, and all those new arrivals see him more clearly—he's nothing but a politician.

His Incumbency offers these people something better than friendship: Pork. Only incumbents, after all, can bring home the bacon. Only they can announce the new grant to study the effects of television on children, or fluoride in water, or airplane noise on milk production—all to be researched and reported right here at good ol' Hometown U.

Maybe it's the new HUD grant for downtown South Succotash (assuming the leading paper in the district is published there). Maybe it's funds to study if we need more open space, a new riverfront park, or special commuter lanes on the interstate. Maybe it's the news that the Department of So-and-So is building a regional office right in his district or that the FAA will add a new runway at the airport. Whatever it is, it comes from hogs, it looks better on TV, shrinks when it's ready to eat (even though everyone loves the sizzle), and is mostly nothing but fat.

Buying votes with pork is His Incumbency's cheapest trick (though the taxpayers pay through the nose). It is, in fact, the most honored tradition of Congress. Some even estimate that as much as half the entire federal budget is pork—expenditures targeted to groups or districts that provide, in return, political support for the pork provider.

Anyone familiar with pork knows, of course, that it spoils. It has be served on time, and that means a few weeks before election. So keep your eyes open for those sizzling announcements in September and October of even-numbered years.

Thus, the fundamentals of incumbency abuse are simple. First, use the frank and the public relations staff to build name identification. Second, use constituent service staff and the computerized correspondence management system to create friendships. Third, use pork to persuade nonfriends that His Incumbency's clout has tangible value. And finally, when all else fails, reinvent reality with television ads.

Congressmen have discovered, like many professional athletes, the wonders of steroids—not the kind of steroids you swallow or stick into your veins to make you a stronger, more powerful, faster, taller, or more muscle-bound athlete, but the steroids you buy in thirty second slots and put on television each election cycle to turn a normal incumbent into a super-congressman or woman.

Congressmen have learned the very simple truth: if they buy more television than their opponent, they will, in almost every case, win reelection. It's almost as simple as that.

His Incumbency, after a few years in office, feels all powerful. As long as he pursues the incumbency strategy successfully and outspends his challengers on steroids, there's hardly any way he can be beaten.

No one can hope to match his name identification or have as many "friends." No one can pretend to have as much power or provide as much pork. No one can extort as much money from special interests to buy the television spots that reinvent his political persona. In fact, only one thing can bring him down: himself.

His Incumbency leaves office only when his desires dictate (or when he is matched against another incumbent or otherwise destroyed by redistricting). Usually his desires tell him to retire or seek higher office. Sometimes other people, his family or doctor (never his staff), dictate such retirement.

But sometimes he leaves because baser desires have produced scandal. His Incumbency develops an immense appetite—for money, for status, for perquisites, for adoration, and even for romance. When he's unable to control these desires, his actions may lead to disgrace of such dimension that his "friends" abandon him, his recognition becomes ridicule, the press parodies his power, and television commercials merely remind the public of his sins.

This is when His Incumbency realizes the shallowness of his political strategy. The press and public, long frustrated by the lack of popular power to challenge the performance or positions of an incumbent, seize at the potential that scandal provides. Every new rumor or disclosure feeds the frenzied mob mentality.

Suddenly, the public can stand up to His Incumbency and defy his arsenal of abuse. Where only a few weeks before everyone had conceded the inevitability of His Incumbency's reelection and paid lip service to his connections, his clout, and his career, now the public mood is rapacious. No longer is he irreplaceable—now he is the subject of mockery and scorn.

Most incumbents know there's a scandal lurking somewhere that can discredit their careers in a flash. But still, the rewards of being the Honorable are so tempting that they cling to Congress like a suckling piglet. They believe that the artistry of their incumbency will preserve the perception of their popularity forever. They hope that no one will look too closely at what Congress has become.

# 5

# WELCOME TO OUR HOUSE

*James K. Coyne was elected to Congress from Pennsylvania's 8th District near Philadelphia in 1980. He defeated incumbent Democrat Peter Kostmayer by a narrow margin the year of Ronald Reagan's first landslide. During his term he served on the Banking and Urban Affairs Committee and the House Administration Committee, which oversees all congressional perquisites. In 1982, his district, altered through redistricting, lost several thousand Republican voters. He was defeated in his reelection bid that year by 2,200 votes out of over 200,000 cast. Peter Kostmayer sits in Congress today, although his 1992 election was put in jeopardy when it was revealed he had written fifty bad checks at the House Bank. The following are some of Jim Coyne's personal recollections of his service in Congress, as seen through the eyes of a citizen legislator.*

I WAS a real novice. No one had expected me to win a seat in Congress in the fall of 1980, and like a newcomer in a poker game who wasn't sure if a flush beat a straight, I suspected that all my new colleagues didn't necessarily have my best interest at heart. But they sure were friendly and tried to make me feel right at home.

Still, I wasn't completely ignorant of how government worked, or was supposed to work. Although I had trained in engineering, economics, and marketing at Yale and Harvard Business School, I had always enjoyed debating issues of public policy. While still in my twenties, I had been invited to join Philadelphia's prestigious Committee of Seventy, a nonpartisan watchdog group that had monitored the fairness of politics and elections in Philadelphia for nearly a century.

In 1978, the committee faced one of its most important challenges when Frank Rizzo proposed a referendum to remove the city's ancient two-term restriction on the office of mayor. Rizzo was a bold and brazen political leader, some would say a tyrant, who probably chuckled when told that the solemn and sedate Committee of Seventy was going to fight his plan to become Mayor for Life.

Living at the time only a few blocks from Independence Hall, I felt that Rizzo's plan was a sacrilege, contrary to the ideals that Philadelphia had celebrated during the national bicentennial only two years earlier. The committee asked me to help lead the campaign to save the city charter with its historic term limitation. My task: Raise money to finance a campaign of radio and television ads against the charter change.

The first lesson I learned was the reality of political fear. Rizzo seemed to relish the role of bully, bragging about his brutality as police chief and proud of photos of himself at a posh political dinner with a nightstick under his cummerbund. Not surprisingly, when citizens and businesses were asked to support the referendum fight, many were afraid to be publicly linked with the struggle. Some were certain that Rizzo would take revenge and, in any case, would rig the elections in such a way that he couldn't be beaten.

Election day proved them both right and wrong. When my wife and I went to cast our votes that morning, the registrar, a Rizzo patron, informed us that we couldn't vote. Their records stated that we had moved out of the precinct to an address a few blocks away, a funeral parlor.

After an appeal to the city's Board of Elections, we finally cast our ballots, but by then the outcome was clear. Rizzo had lost. Philadelphia had turned him down. His political career was over and, in the nation's first modern public referendum on the issue, term limitations had won in a landslide.

Thus, I had some understanding of political careerism when I arrived in Washington in November 1980 as a congressman-elect, but I had little appreciation for the procedures and perquisites of big government. My official political training had been as supervisor of Upper Makefield Township (pop. 3,200), the political jurisdiction encompassing our family's home in Washington Crossing, Pennsylvania.

Upper Makefield's political meeting place was a small room in the back of the township's maintenance garage, illuminated by a pair of 100-watt light bulbs. The supervisors sat at a folding table in front of a dozen or so residents every other Tuesday night to decide what government should do and how to pay for it. For this, I was paid $25 per meeting. There were no perks.

Washington wasn't like Washington Crossing. There were no ordinary citizens there—no neighbors or simple folks. It was full of incumbents, special people who knew they were special. Now, I was a member in this very special club and everyone wanted to make sure I was welcome.

The first call I got the day after the election was from an incumbent from my home state. He demanded that I get down to Washington right away—there was much to learn, plans to make, and a career to start. Most of all, he said, I had to be taught about the perquisites: the staff, the lifestyle, and the travel. In fact, he wanted me to join him on a junket to Europe in January.

I waited a few weeks, nevertheless, to visit Washington, but when I did arrive, the welcome was incredible. A private temporary office was set up for me in a congressional annex and bureaucrats presented an endless list of choices to make about staff, equipment, furniture, and supplies. There was never any question of cost—the working assumption was: Nothing is too good for Congress.

It's not that the trappings of executive life were foreign to me, it's just that I had never seen such extravagant consumption without any awareness of expense. I had been president for nearly a decade of a small family business that was one of the fastest growing firms in the Philadelphia area. Originally an industrial chemical wholesaler, the company had recently branched into high-tech engineering and environmental projects.

Sales had grown to several million dollars, but we still had to focus tightly on the bottom line. For us, a profit of $1\frac{1}{2}$ percent was a good year, so cost control was always a prime consideration. Like most small businessmen, I was constantly looking for ways to improve our productivity and lower costs, while increasing our sales performance and output. And I always knew that any customer was only as happy as his last delivery. In a world where our major competitor had just gone bankrupt, there was no such thing as incumbency advantage.

I had another unusual perspective for a newly elected congressman: I had been trained as an engineer. That meant that solutions had to make sense. Proposals (i.e., hypotheses) had to be tested and performance measured against expectations or design parameters. The historians told me that only eight engineers had been elected to Congress this century. It was, in any case, a lonely point of view.

The lawyers were everywhere. Many of them served on the staff of my principal committee, Banking and Urban Affairs. I quickly learned their idea of what a novice congressman should do. It was simple: shut up and listen to us. I remember one staff member who, after I had attended my first Banking Committee session and asked my first question, ran up to me and said, "But, Mr. Coyne, we didn't give you a question to ask." I began to wonder who really ran things on Capitol Hill.

I soon found out it was the lawyers. Some of them called themselves legislators, others were staff. Still others were lobbyists. There didn't seem to be a big difference. They all ate very well.

They didn't really eat—they grazed. Even before I was sworn in, the invitations arrived. Every night, it seemed, a million shrimp were sacrificed to the Gods of Lobbying at an endless series of ritualistic receptions and fundraisers.

His Incumbency arrives and accepts the beribboned name tag, so no one can mistake him as less than the Honorable nor forget which state or district is his. Quickly he is accosted by the hosts for a few minutes of hollow flattery and praise, a reminder of the group's connections to his district, recollections of their support during his campaign, and remonstrations of their respect and allegiance. Then, he's free to hit the shrimp, the skewered water chestnuts wrapped in bacon, the Chivas, and the caviar. The whole schmooze is over in a flash. Who needs dinner?

A day or two later I went by to see the incumbent who wanted to show me the ropes. We were both from the same state and I suppose he felt it was his duty to introduce me to the joys of incumbency. "Sit down," he said in the brusque but brotherly tone of an impatient upperclassman. "You've got a lot to learn."

"From now on," he advised, "you've got to start acting like a big shot. People are impressed by power and you've got to act like you're powerful. Always travel with an aide driving your car. Always arrive late and let your office visitors cool their heels before they see you. Never place your own phone calls, and remember—you can always call your own shots. You have no boss. You don't have to ask anyone for permission. And whenever you can, ask for more. Never, never settle for what anybody offers you the first time. The voters want you to be greedy for them, so be greedy, and have a good time at their expense."

Then a smile crossed his face as he started to discuss his favorite subject—Perks.

"This place is the greatest place on earth. It's like you're the boss of the biggest business in the world. Any federal employee anywhere will hop when you say "frog," because they know you control their budget and can get them transferred to North Dakota.

"The private sector is even better. They'll give you almost anything you ask. But don't act too grateful—always give the impression that you're slightly disappointed. You don't want them to think that you owe them something."

At this point, I was almost in shock. It's not that I had come to Washington like another Jimmy Stewart in *Mr. Smith Goes to Washington*, but I had expected a bit more decorum in the halls of Their Incumbencies. My new "friend," however, was just warming up to his favorite bit of advice.

"There are a lot of little penny ante perquisites and privileges that everyone thinks are a big deal: the free parking at National Airport, the fancy meals, the gifts, the honoraria, the tickets to all the shows and games. But there's one perk we get that no one can match: the travel. No one gets the special treatment overseas that we do."

It was several months before I found out how right he was. Although I didn't follow his advice and choose a committee assignment that "required" overseas travel, such as Foreign Affairs, Intelligence, Armed Services, or Energy and Commerce, it really didn't matter. This was one House where no one has to stay at home.

*Every* committee has its travel budget. "Ag" committee members *have* to compare farms in Iowa with those in France and Japan. Education and Labor panelists *have* to support trade unionism in Germany and South America. Even members of the Interior Committee *have* to compare our parks with those in Kenya and Switzerland. So, I wasn't too surprised to learn that my principal committee assignment, the Banking and

Urban Affairs Committee, produced an invitation to represent Congress at the annual World Bank meeting.

Royalty never traveled so well. Sure, a first-rate king may have his private yacht and legions of footmen, but Congress has the Air Force's 89th Wing and the U.S. State Department—and they both know who signs the checks.

The 89th Wing is Congress's own airline, based at Congress's own airport, Andrews Air Force Base. Sure, the president shares it with them, but he, at least, has to get Congress to approve his travel allowance. The passengers on Air Congress really do own the airline—and what an airline it is!

Everyone flies first class, and then some. Saluted as you arrive at Andrews Air Force Base, assuming you don't rank direct helicopter taxi service from downtown D.C., you get a courteous military escort to the VIP departure building. No X-ray machines, no lines, no surly ticket agents, just a friendly sergeant to take your bags and show you to your plane (but remember, they're all your planes).

With a fleet of more than a hundred executive jets to choose from, you never find yourself in three-abreast seating. In fact, it's not unusual to have the whole plane to yourself. You are, after all, the reason the whole wing continues to get funded (at more than $150 million per year). It's not surprising then that everyone knows your name.

But all this is mere transportation. The Incumbency treatment doesn't really start until you land. Then you've got a new title—you're part of a CoDel, the five-letter State Department acronym for royal pain in the butt.

The people the State Department assigns to the care and feeding of Congressional Delegations overseas must come from very hardy stock. No one suffers more indignities, accepts more disrespect, or witnesses more examples of unbridled arrogance than these noble, but obsequious, public servants.

The first thing they usually hear is: "Why are you here? Where's the ambassador? Shouldn't he be meeting me at the airport?" Once they explain that the ambassador has a whole country and not just a few junketing Incumbencies to worry about, they promise to make the visit a most memorable one. "Anything you need, don't hesitate to call."

Next, the red diplomatic passports reveal their magic. Customs inspections, as Mrs. Helmsley might have said, are for ordinary people. His Incumbency is whisked through the airport like a rock star. Limousines provide appropriate carriage to the finest hotel, just in time to freshen up for the requisite official dinner, either at our ambassador's residence or as guests of the host country.

Over the next day or two there will be an official schedule to provide a modicum of work product, but the general idea is party, party, party, with sightseeing and shopping to fill in the gaps. It's almost as though the whole system of international diplomacy is just an excuse to justify all the fancy meals, receptions, and ornate edifices without which, apparently, serious bilateral discussions cannot take place.

The best-run committee junkets are those where the "work" is dispensed with in a few lavish lunches and cocktail parties, and the schedule carefully programmed to allow time to hear the opera in Vienna, visit a chateau or two in the Loire Valley, take in the latest play in Piccadilly, or have some custom suits made in Hong Kong. The job of the committee staff is to find a sponsor for each of these extracurricular activities, someone anxious to host a distinguished group of Incumbencies, pick up the tab, and roll out the red carpet.

Usually these affairs include opulent catered dinners in the most elegant settings: A historic mansion in Paris, an intimate wing of their National Art Gallery, or some treasured Imperial Palace reserved for such posh occasions. The only price Their Incumbencies must pay is to listen to a ten-minute introduction of the host, a brief tribute to the sponsors and any of their clients who are along for this impressive ride, and a recitation of the collective set of expectations from the congressional committee. After all, these good people are constituents, too, in the grandest sense of the word.

But, unfortunately, there are usually only eight or nine recesses, known officially as "District Work Periods," that allow enough time to schedule these joyous adventures. Early January, before Congress has any real work, is the best time to head to South America and investigate the menacing drug cartels, perhaps with a stopover in Rio. The Presidents' Day Recess in February is usually an important time to see how the Caribbean Basin Initiative is doing. Easter is the best time to visit Rome or the Holy Land, with necessary refueling stops in Spain or Portugal. Memorial Day reminds many members of the servicemen in Germany or the Far East, and June provides a good time to check our military hardware at the Paris Air Show. The July and August recess is best used for those trips requiring in-depth research, like the ever-popular oversight of the various American bases and possessions in the Pacific Ocean. Australia and New Zealand offer a nice change of pace in the early fall (when it's spring down under), and the weeks between election and News Year's days are there to let you catch anything you might have missed out on earlier—like the grand tour of Eastern Europe, the game preserves of Kenya, or the mandatory visit to the Great Wall of China. So much to give thanks for at Thanksgiving — so many presents to open at Christmas.

When you get back, of course, you have a long list of thank-you notes to write to all those ambassadors who suffered your presence and ego so well. A brief reminder in each of them may be useful to show that you understand their budget request, will work to add $500,000 to the appropriation bill for those necessary improvements in the ambassador's residence, and disallow any staff reductions being proposed by those hard-nosed State Department accountants. So much for homework!

The real work comes when His Incumbency really does have

to go back to his district, though if he's been an incumbent long enough most of this can be delegated to a surrogate congressman on his staff. And while these sojourns among the ordinary voters are necessary to maintain appearances, with artful press and public relations, even these struggles with reality can be relatively painless.

The first rule is keep it short—congressmen in their home district are like house guests and fresh fish: things start to turn bad after three or four days. Like the fish, I suppose, it all depends on how well you're packaged.

Here's where His Incumbency's scheduler saves the day. The object, of course, is to make as many people as possible aware of the fact that the congressman is "home"! Then, he won't have to come "home" so often. The strategy is simple: Get on television and radio, speak to large groups, get involved in some local issue, stage a press event, have a few town meetings to justify all the mail you sent out, schedule a meeting with your biggest contributors, and shake hands wherever you can find the most—in church, at softball games, and at charity events. Members frequently give donations at such events, but they come not from their own pockets but from their campaign treasuries. House Ways and Means Chairman Dan Rostenkowski played a kind of Lady Bountiful for years in his Chicago district, lavishing Polish churches and Hispanic civic groups with hundreds of thousands of dollars in donations from his honoraria income.

Your press staff always does a few days of preliminary carpet-bombing on the local media to promote your presence, and follows up with targeted press releases, recorded radio actualities, and computerized mail to make the memories linger. Do it right and you won't have to do it again for three or four weeks.

The most important rule governing this blitzkrieg approach to incumbent protection is never to let the voters know what you're doing. Some slip. If the definition of a political gaffe is when a member inadvertently tells the truth, then Rep. Joe Kolter of Pennsylvania hit the jackpot in early 1992. The *Pittsburgh Post* published a transcript of a staff meeting he had held.

Rarely has a member been so candid. Kolter called himself a "political whore," who was "here to get elected." He even revealed his favorite campaign tactic: visiting funeral homes. "If I faintly remember who these people are, [I] just walk in and shed a little tear and sign my name and take off."[1] The voters punished Kolter for his inadvertent truthfulness in the 1992 primary: he won only 19 percent of the vote. But defeated congressmen rarely give up. Kolter, ever the political careerist, announced he would run again in 1994 even as he delivered his concession speech.

Still, if members play their advantages right they will rarely encounter the misfortunes of a Joe Kolter. Their district will be so wired that they will have time to enjoy Washington at its best—on the weekend. And nobody does weekends like Washington.

It was Congress, they say, that gave America the five-day work week nearly a century ago. It seems fitting, therefore, that Congress should continue this progress and give itself the five-day weekend. Well, it's not really five days, closer to four and a half, but not bad for now.

It's all part of the big Congressional Lie: Nobody works as hard as we do. The general party line (both parties) is that even though they'd like to be working on important new legislation all week long, they can't wait to return to their districts and be among their thousands of dear friends and neighbors, so they abandon Washington on Thursday night and don't come back until Tuesday morning. Because of this furious schedule, they say, Congress must only work for three days each week, or they won't be able to get "home."

For some *new* members, this schedule reflects reality. For the rest, it creates the World's Best Weekend. Four-day junkets to

Florida, Hilton Head, Aspen, and Vail are one form of The Weekend. Others find comforts closer to home: glamorous spas like the Greenbrier, shows and shopping sprees in New York City, or heavy duty temptations at Atlantic City. But most learn to love the simple charms of our Nation's Capital. Incumbent means "lying down," after all—and here's the best place to do it.

Every weekend is saturated with sophisticated fun for His Incumbency. Embassy parties, posh fundraisers, evenings of witty roasts, or secretive stag nights like the top-rated Alfalfa Club, can keep the tuxedo in use almost any night. Celebrity tournaments, "fun-runs," and Members Only baseball, basketball, tennis, and golf fill in the afternoons.

The private boxes at the Kennedy Center and RFK Stadium are really there for them (as long as the tax laws they write continue to permit their lavish use for lobbying). And all those official government museums, galleries, and palaces of culture around town are careful to invite Congress to every gala event. Thus, we come to understand the real job of His Incumbency's scheduler: RSVP to all those parties. In his own mind His Incumbency is, after all, worth all this treatment. He knows he's one in over half a million, unique in his district. He's as rare as a rock star, and would be as rich as one were it not for his decision to be a "public servant."

Thus, these subsidiary benefits are justifiable and deserved, since he's not being paid what he's really worth. He calculates that he could earn twice as much if he were a lobbyist, though very few ever really do survive in that ultracompetitive profession. But, in any case, he knows that all the good he does, searching for those lost Social Security checks and such, will shield him from history's harsh judgments if anyone criticizes him for a few "moments" of self-indulgence. He is, lest anyone forget, His Incumbency.

# 6

# CHECKS AND BOUNCES

ANNOUNCER: *And now, another Capitol Hill Bank Moment.*

BANK TELLER: *I'm working behind the counter here at the House Bank, when in comes a freshman congressman. He puts $500 into his new checking account. Boy, you should have seen the look on his face when I told him $500 in a Capitol Hill checking account is unheard of. Congressmen never keep that kind of money in the bank.*

CONGRESSMAN: *So this kindly teller tells me that my $500 is worth $60,000 to $100,000 in check-writing privileges! Until that moment I never realized how much I was going to love living in Washington. Heh, heh.*

ANNOUNCER: *Capitol Hill Bank, for worry-free checking. Member F.L.E.E.C.E. A special privilege lender.*

—A satirical ad for the House Bank played
on the Rush Limbaugh Talk Show.

WHEN A MEMBER of Congress walks into the House side of the Capitol, the first thing he passes is the old House Bank just a few feet down the hall from the heavily guarded "Members Only" entrance.

If commercial space were rented in the Capitol, this would be the most sought-after footage. Not only does it have "location, location, location," but this elegant southeast corner of

77

the Capitol is endowed with every imaginable architectural embellishment: marble upon marble, gilt upon brass and bronze, and wonderfully ornate ceilings decorated with hand-painted murals, historical quotations, and political proverbs.

Over the door to the House Bank is a delicately inscribed rubric:

We have built No Temple but the Capitol
We consult no common oracle but the Constitution

No oracle could have predicted that in September 1991, this elegant but overlooked corner of the Capitol would produce the greatest congressional scandal in over a century, setting off a tremor of such magnitude that it could possibly destroy the very foundations of this temple of incumbent privilege and power.

If you were to listen to the excuses from Congress about what the House Bank was, you would think it was little more than a "disbursing office." You might envision a door with "Payroll Dept." stenciled above a grated window, and a little counter where a wrinkled old accountant with a green eye-shade sat and carefully handed out weekly salary checks through an opening in the glass. You would be wrong.

It was a bank—and so much more—but it's unfair to call it the House Bank. It was really the Incumbents' Bank. The institution of the House of Representatives, even its employees and traditions, can't be blamed for what that bank became. It corrupted the Congress because the incumbents corrupted it.

When Jim Coyne was a freshman congressman, the House Bank offered no special fascination. Holly, his wife, was a commercial loan officer with Philadelphia's biggest bank. They both knew what they wanted in banking services, especially when in early 1981 inflation was rampant and bank passbooks were yielding the highest interest rates of the century.

The Sergeant-at-Arms, who oversaw House Bank operations, presented what seemed like a dubious deal. The monthly pay voucher could go directly into the House Bank and he'd provide free checks—but no interest. Alternately, he could deliver an actual paycheck. But he wouldn't deposit the check into any other bank. The House, showing its ignorance here, as in so many other areas, of modern business practice, had yet to discover the concept of Direct Deposit.

A quick review of the competition showed that the Congressional Credit Union, a regular "bank" that served thousands of unelected House employees as well as members, offered what appeared to be a better package: free checks (with a low minimum balance) and interest on an average balance. In addition, the credit union was closer—in the basement of the Longworth House Office Building. No long walk to the Capitol to cash a check was necessary. It was no contest.

The vast majority of members, however, had their paychecks deposited into the House Bank. The most recent GAO audit of June 30, 1991, showed that $20,410,093 was the net salary paid by the Sergeant-at-Arms into members' accounts in the House Bank over the previous twelve months, and that $3,817,892 was paid directly to members by check during the same period.[1]

So why was there a House Bank at all?

Strangely, the Sergeant-at-Arms insisted on giving every member a checking account at the House Bank, even if it wasn't used for payroll deposits. At one level, it was just another privilege and a trivial symbol of His Incumbency's special status that someone else paid for.

The checks from the House Bank were impressive. They looked official, with an engraved American Eagle and the imprimatur of the Sergeant-at-Arms. Some members admitted they looked so beautiful that recipients sometimes didn't cash them, preferring to keep the autographed checks as souvenirs of their historic transaction with Their Incumbencies.

But unbeknownst to freshmen members, or to junior Republicans at least, the House Bank's real reason for existence was to provide other special services not so widely advertised. Its accounts, like so much else about Congress, were unaccountable. Its deficits, like those of our government, weren't a burden to our elected representatives. Its rules, like those our citizens must obey, were always bent for Their Incumbencies. It reflected their reality: It gave them anything they wanted.

The House Bank was the kind of bank an ordinary citizen might dream about. When you walked in, every employee was aware of your presence. There were never any lines—three windows were always ready and the tellers never too busy for you. On the wall, where regular banks have pictures of their founder, president, or board of directors, your picture and those of 434 other members were displayed.

No one has ever gotten money out faster. At the House Bank they never asked to see your driver's license or made you wait while they checked your balance. No worries about out-of-state checks or delays before funds would be available. And, most amazingly of all, no concept of negative numbers.

Some of us may remember studying "imaginary" numbers in high school and college. That must be the kind they used here, numbers that could be turned into a negative amount and still be imaginary. It seems you could have $10 in your House Bank account—in fact, you could never have had more than $10—write a check for $25,000, walk out with the cash, and everything would be just fine.

Ordinary people can only dream about such treatment at their local bank. Members of Congress demand it. They couldn't imagine it any other way. But then none of them ever imagined the nightmare their bank would become.

All the warning signs were ignored, because everyone knew they were as meaningless as the *pro forma* legislative sessions Congress creates every Monday and Friday. Congress is ruthless when it is holding someone else in judgment, but it rarely permits anyone to look over its own shoulder. Only for something as "official" as the House Bank would they even deign to consider a review of their procedures by the General Accounting Office.[2] Thus the GAO audits were reluctantly agreed to by Congress after a 1947 scandal when embezzlement by an employee obligated the U.S. Treasury to bail out the bank to the tune of over $500,000 in today's money.

But an outside review with authority to enforce its recommendations was not something Congress ever allowed, so the House Bank was never audited by the Treasury, the Justice Department, or the IRS. It would show its books only to someone it could ignore, like the General Accounting Office, the Congress's own bookkeeper.

Everyone involved knew what was expected. Congress has a standard operating procedure for things like audits, ethics committees, and standards of official conduct:

1. Congress does whatever it wants
2. Then it asks for a report or audit that purports to review procedures and suspicious activities
3. Makes sure the report looks very official
4. Takes a long time releasing it (the public forgets)
5. Promises to make amends if the report makes recommendations, then ignores them
6. Sends a thank-you letter for the report
7. Keeps everything quiet and out of the papers.

And so the House Bank audit followed the "generally accepted ass-covering principles"(GAAP) for Congress. In fact, it was so easy, it became a regular production number.

In August 1988, the first reported (no one can find an earlier audit) examination of the House Bank produced a mild rebuke for "the lack of check-cashing procedures." Notice it wasn't a question of poor procedures, but rather, no procedures.

The GAO, looking back on this first warning, remarked:

"At the time, we were assured that procedures would be established. Although procedures [subsequently] were drafted, they were not implemented. Sound internal accounting controls would require that written procedures be instituted which would instruct the bank's tellers about matters such as who can cash checks at the bank, what limits are placed on those with check-cashing privileges, and how to handle persons who repeatedly write checks returned due to insufficient funds."

Of course, the tellers knew exactly what the procedures were. Had they been formally written, they would have looked something like this:

—a member can do anything he wants
—a member can cash any check for any amount drawn on any account by anyone at any time, with no questions asked
—it doesn't matter if a member has any or no money in his account
—it doesn't matter how often he has overdrafted his account
—it doesn't matter when he covers his overdraft
—always say "Thank you, Congressman"(or "Mr. Speaker" or "Mr. Chairman" for any of the 170 or so committee and subcommittee chairmen) when you give them the money.

Someone, not surprisingly, decided it wasn't a good idea to put such procedures down in writing, and no one thought it was important to tell the GAO what the procedures really were.

In 1989, Act Two of the drama unfolded when the second audit took place in early August. It took seven months for the

General Accounting Office to produce its eleven-page report and present it to the Speaker and the Sergeant-at-Arms. The two-page letter of transmittal from the comptroller general (the top official of the GAO) didn't even hint at any improprieties. Buried in the report was the following admonition:

> We found that there are no written check-cashing procedures for the tellers at the House Bank to follow [and found] actions occurring which could lead to material losses in the future.

This time, the report included an appendix with the requisite "I-promise-to-fix-everything" letter from House Sergeant-at-Arms Jack Russ:

> I welcome your regular biannual report of the financial statement of the Office of the Sergeant-at-Arms of the United States House of Representatives. While your report concludes that applicable statutes and regulations were complied with, several deficiencies existed with regard to check cashing procedures. I am fully committed to correcting the deficiencies which the General Accounting Office described.

Russ's letter was, of course, a ruse. Not a single procedural reform with regard to member's overdrafts was written or established. Not one member was forced to stop his overdrafts.

His letter ended as follows:

> Again, I appreciate the work and advice provided by the General Accounting Office and believe that we will be able to correct all procedural deficiencies identified in this audit.

By now, the audit procedure was well rehearsed. Everyone knew his part.

Act Three presented the identical cast of characters and began promptly in early August 1990, although the scenes were starting to drag out a bit. This time it was over a year before the GAO published its eighteen-page "Report to the Speaker and the Sergeant-at-Arms of the House of Representatives." The curtain was about to fall on the House Bank. It was September 18, 1991. A Wednesday.

The first five paragraphs of Comptroller General Bowsher's covering letter were almost identical to his earlier transmittal. But there was a bomb hidden at the end:

> Our review [has] revealed that a large number of checks was being cashed at the House Bank and then returned because of insufficient funds. We first informed the Sergeant-at-Arms about this condition in August 1988 and again in our report of February 7, 1990. In commenting on our February 7, 1990, report, the Sergeant-at-Arms stated that check-cashing procedures would be implemented to address the situation. While procedures have been established, they are not being enforced in all cases and have not been effective in reducing the number of checks being returned because of insufficient funds.

Note that the comptroller general does not state that his previous reports were sent to the Speaker, as well as the Sergeant-at-Arms, although they were. Note, too, that he carefully avoids saying that members were writing the bad checks. He seems almost to be blaming the checks themselves for bouncing.

The next day, Tim Burger, a young congressional reporter for *Roll Call*, broke the story. "Members Bounce Thousands of Checks On House Bank, GAO Survey Discovers" was the headline. Soon everyone in the country knew something the incumbents had been hiding. They learned about the House Bank, its special rules, and the way members of Congress took advantage of them. They discovered the real reason for the House Bank.

The House Bank scandal shook the nation because of all that it represents. Not only were members caught with their hands in the cookie jar, but they were caught trying to ignore and then cover up the whole affair. Every imaginable excuse was offered by members to justify the overdrafts, including some that were truly ludicrous.

Some members said it was their wives' fault. Others blamed their staff or accountant. Rep. Duncan Hunter, who wrote 399 bad checks, claimed he was "in moral balance" on the issue because at the same time he was abusing the House Bank he had contributed money to a scholarship fund in his district. Rep. Bob Dornan said he had bounced a $1,000 check because he needed to complete a shrine to the Virgin Mary that he was building in his back yard.

Sergeant-at-Arms Jack Russ attributed the bad checks to the fact that the pay of members had not risen fast enough, "forcing" some of them to "run $1,000 behind." Bill Alexander, a powerful member of the Appropriations Committee, offered this remarkable explanation: "To put this [his 487 overdrafts] in the simplest terms, I have been broke for the last six years, and even though I found it difficult to make ends meet, I have always stayed within the rules of the House disbursing office."[3]

The GAO's complaint, of course, was that there *were* no rules. It is reassuring that a distinguished legislator such as Bill Alexander who decides how the taxpayers' money is spent was able to obey nonexistent rules, bounce 487 checks, and be broke on a salary of $125,100. Such "experience" must surely help him and other members better understand our budget deficit.

Ever since September 19, 1991, the leadership of the House has been declaring that the House Bank scandal "is over." Speaker Foley went onto the House floor and argued that no member had broken the law and that it was, in any case, not the taxpayers' money. Each successive revelation shows that the scandal won't be over until the House undergoes fundamental change. Congress has become THE scandal, the bank merely a symbol.

Congress must first change its concept of privilege. To serve in Congress is a citizen's most fundamental privilege. That should be enough.

Congress must change its concept of power. Its power flows from those they represent. It must not be abused.

Congress must change its concept of the congressional career. Members must balance their personal ambition with an understanding of political equity.

Congress must come to accept some rules, some limits. Until then, there are no checks. Until then, the future of a disgraced Congress hangs in the balance.

# 7

---

# CONGRESS AS A CAREER

---

*Congress has become a professional legislature, where members come early, stay late, and die with their boots on.*

—Former Rep. BILL FRENZEL of Minnesota.

MOST MEMBERS OF CONGRESS oppose term limits with a lot of rhetoric about letting the people vote for whom they want. But their real reasons are often far more personal. As leader of a term limit organization and former member of Congress, one of us is well known on Capitol Hill. One day, we were accosted at a shopping center by a congressman's genuinely terrified spouse. "You have to stop doing this term limit campaign!" she exclaimed. "What else can my husband do? You're trying to take his job away!" As it turned out, her husband's congressional career *was* cut short, but not by term limits. He retired after it was discovered he had written hundreds of bad checks at the House Bank.

That congressional spouse isn't alone in wanting to hang on at all costs to the trappings of pomp and power on Capitol Hill. Take Rep. Bob Davis, a Republican congressman from Michigan who was forced to retire in 1992 after it was revealed he had written 878 bad checks at the House Bank. The week before he announced his retirement, he called up Matt

Wirgau, a GOP political activist, to discuss his decision. Davis was an emotional wreck, at times nearly sobbing into the phone. "Politics is the only thing I know how to do," he told Wirgau. "I don't know what I can possibly do after leaving Congress. Do you know what I was before going into politics? A mortician! I can't go back to that!"

More and more members of Congress view their jobs as part of a political career, and probably the best one to which they can aspire. Members who think of politics as a lifelong vocation are a new and unfortunate trend in politics. The sociologist Max Weber once noted that the rise of bureaucratic government occurred when the number of people who lived "for" politics (namely viewing it as an avocation) became smaller than the number who lived "off of" politics and viewed it as a career.

The Founding Fathers believed that congressmen should have a vocation in the larger outside world. They recognized that most Americans want to perform their civic duty, but then want largely to forget about politics and get down to the serious business of living. A well-rounded life for most people is centered around raising a family, building a career, being active in church and social groups, and engaging in self-improvement, not with being obsessed by a concern with politics and governing other people's lives.

Voluntary term limits were part of the American political tradition for more than a hundred years. The Founding Fathers wanted a citizen legislature comprised of men such as the Roman hero Cincinnatus, who left his plow to raise an army to defend Rome. He returned victorious and could have easily become a dictator. Instead, he once again became a common citizen. The ideal politician was someone who served a few terms and went home, perhaps to run for another office after some experience with everyday life. At the time of the Civil War, less than 2 percent of the House served more than twelve years. Today many members seek the same job security granted to federal judges. In the current Congress, 34 percent of members have spent more than twelve years in office, and many have been committee chairmen that long.

The only way for an outsider to get elected at present is to wait for the holder of a seat to leave it. But even then new blood is sometimes blocked from entering the system. Today, when a seat opens up, a leading candidate for it will often be a *former* member of Congress, desperate to get back inside the Beltway. "The fever's got me, and the only cure is Congress," said Dan Marriott of Utah in 1990, the year he tried to get back his old seat.[1] Such statements contributed to his defeat, but no doubt he is still nursing his fever and hoping for a return engagement.

Soon after a member leaves, he finds that life just isn't the same with the folks back home. After losing a 1982 Senate race, Rep. David Emery spent five years in Washington as an arms-control negotiator. He finally went back to Maine in 1988 to try business consulting, but didn't like it. "When you've been in public policy for a long time, it's a rather difficult transition," he told *Roll Call*, the Capitol Hill newspaper. The voters weren't willing to help out. Emery lost his 1990 comeback attempt.

Some former members are so bitten by the Washington bug that they try to return again and again. Take California Rep. John Rousselot, first elected to Congress in 1960 at age thirty-three. Gerrymandered out of his seat two years later, he returned to his public relations business. In 1970, he moved, ran from another district, and returned to Congress. In 1982, another gerrymander ended his second congressional career. Ten years later, when a court-drawn redistricting plan created a new district in the Los Angeles County desert, he tried to start a *third* congressional career at age sixty-five. "He's an old warhorse, and he can't stand being put out in the political pasture," says John Allen, a political activist from the area.[2] Mr. Rousselot finished with a humiliating 7 percent of the vote in the Republican primary.

Some former members have other reasons for pining for a return to Capitol Hill. Just after he announced his 1990 plans to run for his old seat, former GOP Rep. Bob Price of Pampa, Texas, admitted the previous year's congressional pay raise had motivated him. He brazenly told *Roll Call*: "Congress voted themselves 125,000 bucks. I can't make that much around here."

The tendency of elected officials to view themselves as special and above their fellow citizens isn't limited to those serving in Congress or state legislatures. Dr. Robert Supers was elected in 1988 to a four-year term on the city council of Clovis, California, a city of 54,000 near Fresno. For two years he served as mayor pro tem. He had a distinguished career on the council, and would have been an easy favorite for reelection. Yet he chose not to run a second time and stepped down in April 1992.

"I enjoyed the heck out of my service on the council," he admits. "That's part of the problem. Serving in public office is very seductive, and it's easy to lose your perspective if you are there too long." He recounts how even a city council member in a medium-sized city can imagine he is an exalted figure. Council members, he notes, are placed on a dias that raises them literally above everyone else in the council room. "I was constantly surrounded by people who were very deferential to me and wanted to do me favors," he recalls. "They all wanted something." Letters to him from the governor and other important officials addressed him as "The Honorable."

Supers says that kind of recognition bothered him. "I'm proud of my standing in the community as a medical doctor. But that is because I have worked hard to establish expertise in an area, and I do enjoy being recognized for that. But what bothered me about public office was that I was immediately viewed as an expert on all public policy issues just because I was there. If you are told that often enough, pretty soon you begin to believe it."

Supers believes that with term limits, elected officials will have to return at least periodically to live among the people and directly experience the impact of the laws they have written. "Farmers turn over the soil every year because they know it makes for better crops," he notes. "We need to do the same thing for politicians."[3]

Serving in office used to be viewed by many Americans as something akin to jury duty. You took your turn at passing laws for the benefit of all and then passed the gavel to someone else. Of course, politics in America has always had its share of scheming, grasping officeholders; outright bribery is probably less common today than in the days of Tammany Hall. But what is different about politics today is its careerist bent. For most officeholders, politics is now a job for people who decided early in life to pursue that line of work. Congress, state legislatures, and even city councils are filled with people who probably served in their high school student council. Ed Crane of the Cato Institute tells the story of a 1990 debate on term limits he had with Mike Roos, then assistant majority leader of the California Assembly. Roos's argument against term limits was the embodiment of incumbent arrogance. He explained that he had spent thirteen years serving the people of his district, and that having been returned to office again and again had nothing to do with the advantages of incumbency. He resented, he said, the concept of term limits because he had always wanted to be a legislator. In fact, he had studied public administration in college in pursuit of that goal. "I've been training to do this job for all of my life," he stated. "This is my life and my career, and you're trying to take it away from me."

Crane told Roos that he had no doubt of his sincere desire to stay in politics. "But that is not the kind of ambition or the kind of person we want making decisions concerning the rest of us, who are more inclined to live and let live." Crane added wryly that a substitute for term limits might be a proposal to bar from public office anyone who had ever run for student government in high school.

Henry Olsen is now a Philadelphia lawyer, but he originally wanted a political career in his home state of California. In college he became an expert at gerrymandering: the arcane art of drawing districts that help one party at the expense of another. By age twenty-two, he was an influential staffer for the Republican minority in the State Assembly. Then in 1986, at the age of only twenty-six, he launched his own campaign for a vacant state assembly seat in San Jose.

"I was a principled conservative, but I was addicted to the game of politics," he recalls. "But even so, I wondered about running for office at such a young age. Here I was, barely out of school, and yet because of my work in the state capital I had an excellent chance to win because I was so adept at technical politics. I had access to a vast network of political contributors and direct mail companies. I was better prepared to run for office by having been a legislative staffer than many people who had been active in my community for twenty years."

Because of his contacts, Olsen was able to raise over $250,000 and run a professional campaign. He wound up losing by a few percentage points to another political junkie who was ten years older and even more skilled at running for office. "Looking back on it, I'm glad I lost," Olsen remarks. "I would have gone to Sacramento as a complete political animal. The voters would have been better served if I'd led a real life first in my community, married, raised a family, and been active in local groups. I would have been a much more well-rounded legislator."[4]

Olsen realized the political system needed reform when he saw how much it had been taken over by professionals like himself. Dan Walters, a columnist for the *Sacramento Bee*, agrees and says one of the benefits of term limits in California will be that "once again there will be room for people who want to get elected, accomplish a specific goal, and then get out of town."[5]

Unlike Henry Olsen, Dennis Brown did win a seat in the California legislature. In 1978, the young stockbroker upset a Democratic incumbent who had gone against that year's popular tax-cutting Proposition 13. He was twenty-nine, and only four years out of business school.

During his twelve years in the legislature, Brown saw new colleagues arrive and become completely captured by the system. "There's nothing like Congress, but the California legislature is the closest thing to it," said Democratic Assemblyman Ted Lempert, explaining why he was running for Congress at the age of thirty after term limits cut short his legislative career.[6] In the late 1980s, California's legislature was pure heaven for professional politicians. It employed 2,800 staffers and was besieged by influential lobbies bidding for its favors. It's no wonder California voters slapped a strict term limit on the legislature in 1990, along with deep budget cuts.

Dennis Brown recalls that when he served in the legislature, "the atmosphere was so heady that many members bought into it completely. The people they cared about most were their colleagues and the lobbyists. Local officials got some of their attention, but constituents with concerns were viewed as an irritant by many legislators." Brown was elected to his party's second-highest leadership position, but became disillusioned quickly. "The most important thing for most members I knew was to get reelected," he recalls.

Brown went through a spiritual reawakening during his last term, and he decided to retire in 1990. He promptly became a missionary for his church in Cambodia. "It was very important for me to become involved with people on a more genuine level after being in the unreal world of politics for so long," he says. He returned to California in early 1992, just as a new redistricting plan redrew the congressional district he lived in and forced the incumbent to retire. Dennis Brown lost his Republican primary for Congress by 105 votes, but he remains a firm supporter of term limits. "They make all politicians realize they have a finite time to get things done, and it makes them not think of their office as a career," he notes. "I don't know of anyone who wouldn't benefit from that knowledge."[7]

Vin Weber was another political golden boy. Growing up in rural Minnesota, he became active in Republican politics in his teens. While still in his midtwenties, he was campaign manager for Rudy Boschwitz when he won a landslide victory for the U.S. Senate in 1978. Two years later, at age twenty-eight, Vin Weber was elected to the U.S. House in his own right and became one of that body's most respected members. He retired in 1992 after revealing he had written 125 bad checks at the House Bank.

Weber had always been a firm opponent of term limits, but the legislative gridlock and scandals of 1991 have made him reconsider. "In my conversations with other members in the wake of the bank scandal, I was struck by how many of them had a careerist mentality," he recalls. "They were worrying about being defeated and couldn't possibly imagine doing anything other than serving in Congress. I found that attitude kind of sad. Certainly, the career orientation of many members explains why so few of them take political risks or propose bold programs."[8]

Weber has softened his opposition to term limits. He used to favor a longer term of four years for House members so that a president might be more likely to have a working majority in

Congress. Now, he is willing to balance that loss of voter control with a limit on the number of four-year terms a member could serve.


Should Bill Clinton not be elected president, it would be in part because he couldn't shake his nickname: "Slick Willie." Too many voters saw him as a career politician too skilled for his own good in the art of manipulation. Clinton has admitted he has always hungered for a political career. In his famous letter to the Arkansas ROTC colonel who allowed him to escape the draft, the twenty-three-year-old Clinton wrote that he had finally decided to become eligible for the draft "for one reason: to maintain my political viability within the system." He already viewed himself as following in the footsteps of John F. Kennedy. "For years I have worked to prepare myself for a political life characterized by both practical political ability and concern for rapid social progress." As columnist Paul Gigot points out, those were not the words of your average ambitious twenty-three year old.

Since his days as a student, Clinton has devoted himself exclusively to politics. Immediately after graduating from Yale Law School at age twenty-seven, he ran for Congress and won 48 percent of the vote against a Republican incumbent. Two years later he was elected attorney general of Arkansas. But he didn't warm that chair long. In 1978, he became at thirty-two the youngest governor in his state's history. When he was defeated for reelection in 1980, he made a *pro forma* stab at being a lawyer, but in reality he spent almost all his time on the comeback trail. After retrieving the governorship in 1982, he never surrendered it again. Instead, he immediately began planning to run for president.

But even Bill Clinton recognizes the cost he has paid for his relentless pursuit of political power. "Compulsive politicians," he told reporter Joe Klein, are "probably not far from" compulsive drug addicts like his half-brother Roger.[9] Many voters picked up on Clinton's single-minded need for elected office and power, and in a year when professional politicians have fallen below used car salesmen in the public's esteem, it's no surprise that many voters in the primaries rejected him even after he had locked up the nomination. The very qualities that have allowed him to muscle his way to the Democratic nomination have convinced many voters he is unworthy of the presidency.

George Bush is also a professional politician, though he at least waited until he was forty before first running for office in 1964. Since then, he has held a political job for all but six of the ensuing twenty-eight years, and at least three of those were spent on the campaign trail. Holding office is very important to him, as David Frost learned when President Bush told him that "he would do anything he had to in order to win reelection."

Today, Congress is filled with people like Bill Clinton and George Bush. One would think that having developed their impressive incumbent protection machine and seen reelection rates in the 95 percent to 98 percent range during the 1980s members would take more risks in public policy. Nothing could be further from the truth. Members who couldn't be dislodged from their seats short of an earthquake frantically try to suppress competition and campaign as if defeat were right around the corner. House Speaker Tom Foley explained the thinking behind this behavior in Alan Ehrenhalt's pathbreaking book, *The United States of Ambition*. Today's professional politician, Foley said, is a sort of political athlete, obsessed with campaigning and doing well, no matter how feeble the opposition. Members, Foley added, "have an abundance of ego strength, a certain amount of competitiveness, and a willingness to tolerate pain in order to achieve a goal. It doesn't fall into your lap. They are in that sense more driven than members were in the past."[10]

Members run scared because the prospect of losing is truly awful—for the most part, the end of a lifelong career in politics. One conservative Republican congressman apologized to us recently for taking a cowardly stand on an issue. But, he assured us, if he should win a fourth term in 1994, he would become more politically courageous. When asked to explain he replied, "In 1992 I will get a completely safe seat in redistricting, and in 1994 I'm finally vested in my congressional pension and won't have to look over my shoulder all the time." Don't hold your breath waiting for that member to become a Profile in Courage.

On the rare occasions when a member does lose he or she often describes the experience as similar to a death in the immediate family. Democratic Rep. Jerry Patterson recounted how he felt after he was defeated for reelection in 1984. "When your voting card doesn't work anymore, it hits you. The first week or so you go through a mourning period. The first stage is disbelief or denial. You just don't believe it could happen to you. Then you go through a stage when you're angry at yourself, maybe other people, the voters who didn't return you, and mostly at the person who defeated you. Then you come up with excuses why you lost. The fourth stage is depression. You cross the street to avoid talking to someone coming your way. You don't return your phone calls because you don't want to be hurt again. The last stage, the fifth stage, is acceptance."[11]

Even current members of Congress confess the drawbacks of long, uninterrupted service in office. "There is a burnout problem," explains Rep. Andy Jacobs, a Democrat from Indiana. Mr. Jacobs, who was first elected in 1964, says he became a better member after he was defeated in 1972 and forced into private life for two years. "When I came back, I felt as if I was more one of the people," he recalls. Still, he has never gotten off the treadmill again and has now served eighteen years in his *second* stint on Capitol Hill. One of the reasons he supports term limits, he says, is that they would force members to take a sabbatical and return to private life. Because the seat would open up again in a few years, they would have a good chance of returning to office with a new perspective. Under the current system, members are fearful of leaving. "They know the seat might not open up for twenty years," says Jacobs. "They also have a phobia about their ability to earn a living. They don't realize their talents, and how much they could contribute in other areas."[12]

While there are many talented people in Congress, the talents of some have been honed strictly to the art of getting elected. Those talents—speaking ability, public-relations skills, a distinctive personality—can get a person into Congress, but they often make him completely unsuited to the task of legislating. Consider Ed Koch, who was a congressman from New York for nine years before becoming mayor of New York. As mayor he thrived as an administrator, but he realized he had been an inattentive legislator. He discovered the burdensome nature of the federal regulations he had worked for, the waste he had promoted, and the abuse to which many programs he had supported were prone. He apologized to his former constituents for his voting record in Congress, and took to calling himself "Mayor Culpa." "I didn't understand what I was doing when I served in Congress, because in Congress you spend other people's money," he confessed.[13]

Term limits will also change the types of people who run for office. "A Congress without a career path would be a healthy mix of old idealists and young fogeys," predicts Rep. Andy Jacobs of Indiana. There would be fewer people running for reasons given by Rep. Jim McDermott, a Democrat from Washington State, who told a group of lobbyists in June 1991, "After I left the state legislature in 1987, I was burned out and didn't want any more of politics. The reason I decided to come back and run for Congress in 1988 is because I knew I would have a safe seat after the incumbent retired."[14]

In a survey of California legislators, about one-third said they would not have run for office the first time had term limits been in effect.[15] An analysis of the candidates running for the first post-term limit legislature in California in 1992 found that 28 percent fewer candidates described themselves as lawyers than in 1990. The number of people in business running for office in 1992 increased by 17 percent.

Many people believe it is no longer possible for "citizen legislators" to handle the complex affairs of modern government. Nelson Polsby, for example, says, "It is a delusion to think that good public servants are a dime a dozen in each congressional district, and that only the good ones would queue up to take their twelve-year fling at congressional office."[16]

This is absurd. It is the height of arrogance to assert that there are not many fine men and women all over America who could be outstanding leaders. When this country was in its infancy, the state of Virginia had roughly the same population as one U.S. House district has today. Yet it produced George Washington, Thomas Jefferson, James Madison, George Mason, and many other giants.

No doubt readers of this book could sit down and list at least five or six people in their district who would make great members of Congress. Now, imagine yourself asking those people, "Will you run for Congress?" Almost all of them would probably answer, "You've got to be kidding. No logic would lead me to take on an incumbent congressman knowing that it would cost me thousands of dollars, take up a year of my life, expose me to all sorts of outrageous campaign tactics, and, when it's all over, result in certain defeat. And even if by some fluke I did win, I would have to wait years to build up enough seniority to make a real difference. No thanks."

If amateurs in government practice politics in order to make policy, the professional politicians do precisely the opposite. Policy considerations are subordinate and subservient to the advance of their political careers, which are the dominant motivating factors in their lives.

The most important political reform we can make is to reduce the ranks of the amoral political technocrats in office and enlarge the numbers of legislators for whom a political career is an interlude and an opportunity for public service.

# 8

## THE STAFF INFECTION

*Today's Hill staffers write most of the legislation and speeches, they do all kinds of work that the members of Congress should be doing. In fact, it is safe to say that the U.S. Congress is now run by paid staffers, not by people elected to do the job.*

—Former Senator BARRY GOLDWATER (R.-Ariz.)[1]

*I heard a senator the other day tell me another senator hadn't been in his office for three years; it is just staff. Everybody is working for the staff, staff, staff, driving you nutty, in fact.*

—Senator ERNEST HOLLINGS (D.-S.C.)[2]

SENATORS GOLDWATER AND HOLLINGS AREN'T the only ones in Washington complaining about the "shadow government" of congressional staffers. There are presently more than 37,000 congressional employees, a work force the size of two army divisions. As recently as 1970, there weren't enough to form even one. No other legislative body in the world has so many employees; Canada, with 3,500, is the runner-up.

The vast majority of staffers are bright, energetic, and well meaning. For most, Capitol Hill means long hours at menial tasks for mediocre pay in crowded, unsafe workspaces that would be closed down by any health inspector if Congress hadn't exempted itself from all labor laws.

At the heart of this invisible congressional army are the fifteen thousand people who work on personal or committee staffs, some thirty for each member. In 1970 there were only ten per member. Ironically, as the number of staffers, or "hill rats," has skyrocketed Congress's legislative productivity has slowed; many of the staffers bump into each other because of the overlapping jurisdiction of committees. Congress is like a failing railroad: the less freight it carries the more people it employs.

All of the featherbedding on Capitol Hill is for a single purpose: to make members look good and stay elected. John Jackley, who worked for seven years as press secretary to House Majority Whip-at-Large Ronald Coleman, wrote in his book *Hill Rat,* "The members, those 435 Gods Who Walk, always come first. And the true Hill Rat's credo is, 'Ask not what your member can do for the issue, but rather what the issue can do for your member.' " Jackley says that all staffers have one thing in common: "They all sport that 'Christ-please-no-constituents-today' sneer, and they have that knowing walk, that here-I-come, ready-or-not, three-piece-suited swagger that says here be Hill Rats, and they be bad."[3]

It's no wonder Ladislaw Giericki, a member of Poland's Solidarity movement who interned for a congressman in 1990, couldn't believe his eyes when he saw the swarms of hill rats on Capitol Hill. He remembers his experience in Congress as a sobering lesson in the failings of American democracy. When he was told that the U.S. Senate was preparing to send over a group of staffers to show the Polish Parliament how to organize itself he was stunned. "We have to learn from your mistakes as well as your successes," he insisted. "I could not believe the number of congressional aides who pulled the strings of their bosses."[4]

In reality, the number of Capitol Hill staffers with real influence number only a few hundred, and even those are almost unknown save to Washington insiders. A $250 volume called the *Almanac of the Unelected* has been published as a guide to the 650 or so congressional aides lobbyists should invite to lunch. Whereas executive branch officials can't accept a cup of coffee from a business contact, some top congressional staffers would be insulted if a "fact-finding" junket weren't part of the deal. And, of course, many staffers do a lucrative business speaking to trade associations and other "interested parties" in legislation. In 1989, Kevin Gottlieb, a key figure in the Keating Five scandal, made some thirty speeches while he was staff director for the Senate Banking Committee—a few at $600 each—for a single organization called Washington Campus. He earned more money from speaking fees in 1989 than his Senate bosses could legally make.[5]

Staffers who leave Capitol Hill, moreover, often hit the jackpot as high-priced lobbyists and consultants. The Senate's retiring Sergeant-at-Arms traded in his $97,000 government salary for an estimated $300,000 salary with the Washington lobbying firm of Cassidy & Associates.[6]

These upper-crust staffers represent a kind of shadow government in Washington. Many have accumulated so much power that they can "micromanage" the executive branch, often dictating the most minute details of daily governance and subjecting officials to continual investigation. In 1989, some congressional staffers slapped personnel restrictions on the Department of Justice's budget: the department was flatly prohibited from transferring any of its employees as part of an internal reorganization. The real purpose was to keep the department from shutting down a two-man FBI office in Butte, Montana. The FBI office stayed put, and the staffers' boss was no doubt happy. But the cost was high. Then-Attorney General Dick Thornburgh claimed the rule made it impossible for him to reorganize his department's strike force on organized crime.

Some staffers have come to feel they have more power than members of Congress. That's why only a few ever run for office themselves. One Senate staffer who eventually did run was Rep. Norman Dicks, Democrat of Washington. A year after his election he said, "People asked me how I felt about being elected to Congress, and I told them I never thought I'd give up that much power voluntarily."[7]

Mr. Dicks' dependence on staff is inevitable given the topsy-turvy growth of congressional involvement in American life. One reason staffers are so important is that members collect committees the way some people collect baseball cards. In the Senate, the average member has a seat on 4.8 of the regular standing committees and sits on more than twelve subcommittees. More than two-thirds of the Democrats in the House and Senate chair a committee or subcommittee; each has its power base and source of campaign contributions. "You get spread like very cheap margarine on grocery store white bread. The taste isn't there after a while," reports Rep. Dennis Eckart, a retiring Democrat from Ohio.[8]

On a typical day, a member of Congress has two and sometimes three committee hearings, meetings, and floor votes occurring simultaneously. He will rush in late to one hearing, be briefed by a staffer who has monitored it, deliver his sound-bites for the TV cameras, and then run to the next committee hearing. This ludicrous routine prompted Democratic senator Bob Kerrey of Nebraska to make congressional reform a major plank in his campaign for president in 1992. He proposed to reduce the number of congressional committees by an eye-popping 75 percent, and the number of legislative staff by 35 percent.[9]

Kerrey has seen how some staffers often function so closely with their bosses that they become virtual alter egos. Retiring

GOP Sen. Warren Rudman put it bluntly, "I know too many people who rely totally on staff, and never even argue with them."[10] Congressmen tend to fear substance as a savage fears science, economist Tom DiLorenzo noted.[11]

Michael Malbin, who now directs the Rockefeller Institute of Government in Albany, N.Y., recalls going to interview then-Rep. John Kluczynski, chairman of a subcommittee on public works. He wanted details on a $23 billion transportation bill. The congressman asked if a staffer could sit in on the meeting in case Malbin had "technical" questions. Malbin agreed, and after the staffer arrived posed his first query: "What makes this issue so important?" Chairman Kluczynski answered, "This is a tremendously important bill. It involves millions of dollars." Kluczynski then turned to the staffer and said, "No, billions, isn't it?"

In truth, few committee chairmen come close to being that vacuous, but the tangle of overlapping responsibilities makes it inevitable that many staffers become, in effect, surrogate legislators. Treatment for drug abuse is handled by an amazing thirteen congressional committees or subcommittees.

Staffers played a key role in the S&L scandals that will wind up costing the nation over $400 billion. In 1989, the Senate Ethics Committee investigated the activities of Charles Keating and the five senators he recruited as errand boys to do his bidding. But it didn't stop there. During the hearings, Sen. Alan Cranston of California admitted that his top banking aide, Carolyn Jordan, had inserted material favorable to Keating into the *Congressional Record* without his knowledge. Jordan had been a guest of Keating's at his palatial Phoenician Hotel in Phoenix, Arizona.

Keating also courted other influential staffers. Curtis A. Prins, top banking aide to Rep. Frank Annunzio, was high on the list because Annunzio chaired the House Subcommittee on Financial Supervision and had been a fierce critic of the regulations that have brought S&L high flyers down to earth.

In March 1987, Prins and former Rep. David Evans, then a Keating lobbyist, flew to California and Arizona to inspect Keating's investment properties. They stayed at the posh Crescent Hotel for free, had dinner at Keating's home, and played golf at his expense. They even took Keating's corporate jet to Las Vegas for a junket, which Evans paid for.

Prins reported all this activity on his financial disclosure form as a visit to "savings and loans to discuss recapitalization legislation." His disclosure notes that all expenses were paid by David Evans, though it makes no mention of the side trip to Las Vegas. Prins claimed he repaid Evans in cash for that. Confronted with the lavish treatment he accepted from Keating, Prins replied, "Keating snookered me. I wasn't the only one."[12]

Sometimes staffers don't even have to work on Capitol Hill to influence legislation. And sometimes the legislators can line their very own pockets, not merely those of wealthy special interests.

Take the case of Section 89, a notorious measure that became part of the 1986 Tax Reform Act after two Treasury Department staffers, Kent Mason and Harry Conaway, decided companies should be forced to prove that their employee fringe benefits weren't skewed in favor of higher-salaried workers. They drafted the legislation and somehow persuaded House Ways and Means Chairman Dan Rostenkowski to fold it into the tax reform bill without a single hearing or official sponsor.[13] The effects were horrendous. Congressional analysts estimated that Section 89 would pile on the nation's employers some 22,000 worker years of paperwork and prove so costly that some companies would drop fringe benefits altogether.

Yet this loopy provision became law without anyone noticing. Democratic Rep. John LaFalce, chairman of the Small Business Committee, admitted, "I have not talked to any member of Congress who says he understood what Section 89 was all about, or even that there was a Section 89."[14] It's little wonder that staffers in Washington sometimes say they have the power of members without the accountability.

Shortly after Section 89 passed, Kent Mason, one of the Treasury aides, was suddenly hired by the Joint Committee on Taxation, cochaired by none other than Representative Rostenkowski. But both Mason and Conaway soon left government completely. They were hired by firms where their duties included interpreting for clients the Section 89 tax law they had parachuted into the tax code. A consulting group began marketing a $5,500-a-copy Section 89 software program, which they said was "reviewed/designed," as well as endorsed and recommended, by none other than "Kent Mason, who wrote Section 89." It seems writing your own laws in Washington can be lucrative as well as fun.

But such riches can be fleeting. The uproar over Section 89 and its curious pedigree forced Congress to repeal it in late 1989.

Still, much of the handiwork of behind-the-scenes staffers survives and is law today. Sometimes staffers barely out of college sweatshirts write their whims into legislation. Peter Osterlund, who reports on Congress for the *Baltimore Sun*, says that no employer on earth gives its junior aides so much responsibility at such a young age as Congress. Osterlund recalls the case of Kathleen Bertelsen, who in 1982, at the age of twenty-four, dictated the level of U.S. aid to Lebanon.

Ms. Bertelsen worked for a freshman Democrat named Sam Gejdenson who was assembling an emergency aid package for Lebanon. The bill was supposed to be dropped off at the House chamber before everyone left for the weekend. Bertelsen ran the supposedly finished bill to the House floor and left it with Democratic Rep. Toby Moffett. "Wait!" cried

Moffett, as Bertelsen began to leave. The bill didn't specify how much money was supposed to go to Lebanon. What aid amount should he write in?

Bertelsen began to think, "Okay, I'm twenty-four, and this is foreign policy." She considered various numbers, ranging from $10 million to $100 million. "Forget it," she thought, "just pick a nice-sounding number."

"How about $25 million?" she blurted. Moffett scribbled down the figure and dashed into the chamber. A few nights later President Reagan announced the U.S. would send $20 million in aid to Lebanon—a slight cut from the figure she had dictated. Ms. Bertelsen went on to become a key staffer on an international trade subcommittee.

Anyone who doesn't believe staffers exercise that kind of power on a day-to-day basis should talk to Mark Bisnow, a former aide to such senators as Hubert Humphrey and Bob Dole. "Just watch senators on their way into the chamber for a vote," he says. "Many will quickly glance to the side where aides stand compressing into a single gesture the sum of information their bosses need: thumbs up or thumbs down."[15]

In 1990, Bisnow joined the private sector and wrote an article that called for slashing congressional staffs in half. He was quickly attacked in a speech by Rep. Patricia Schroeder, who heads the House Committee on Civil Service. When Bisnow called her office to discuss the issue, his call was returned by a staffer who informed him that he really should talk with Andy Feinstein, the committee staffer who had written her remarks and was the only one who could address the issue. "I felt that was confirmation of everything I had written," Bisnow said.[16]

# 9

# TERM LIMITS ARE
# AN AMERICAN TRADITION

IF THE PHILOSOPHY behind our American system of government could be expressed in a single sentence, it would be Lord Acton's: Power corrupts. The whole structure of our government is designed to limit power. It is why we have a federal, rather than a national, system of government. It is why the government is divided into three separate but equal branches. It is why we have a bicameral legislature. The concept of term limits was well known to our Founding Fathers. It was as hotly debated during the founding of our country as it is today.

Term limits, then, aren't a new idea. They have made a comeback because the reality of today's politics makes them necessary. Something must be done to contain the damage caused by the "permanent government" of career politicians in charge of our Congress and most state legislatures.

Over the years, term limits for Congress have been endorsed by the likes of Thomas Jefferson, Abraham Lincoln, Harry Truman, Dwight Eisenhower, and John F. Kennedy. Ike left office saying that if a limit on office was good for the president it would probably be good for Congress.

But the history of term limits goes back much farther, many

hundreds of years before the Constitution. Its roots are in that earliest of democracies, ancient Athens.[1]

The spirit of civic virtue flowered in Athens. Pericles, the father of Greek democracy, convinced his fellow Athenians that they should demand greatness both from their leaders and from themselves. A statesman was someone who could "know what must be done and be able to explain it; to love one's country and be incorruptible."

The Athenians imposed one of the most severe term limits on their governors. Men held office for only one year before they had to rotate with someone else. And ten times within that year, they could be voted out by a majority of the roughly six thousand Athenians in the assembly.

Until the first century B.C., the Roman republic rotated tribunes and various magistrates, including their consuls, by confining them to one year in office. No one could serve a second term unless he had been out of office for ten years. In the republic of Venice the inner circle rotated annually, while in Florence the top officials were limited to a single term of two months.[2]

Rotation in office was popular as well among many of the thinkers of the Enlightenment, several of which directly influenced the patriots who fought in the Revolutionary War against Britain. Perhaps the finest expression of pro-term limit sentiment—then called "rotation in magistry"—was penned by two Englishmen, John Trenchard and Thomas Gordon, in their classic revolutionary era pamphlet, "Cato's Letters":

"Men, when they first enter into magistracy, have often their former condition before their eyes. They remember what they themselves suffered with their fellow subjects from the abuse of power, and how much they blamed it; so their first purposes are to be humble, modest and just; and, probably, for some time, they continue so. But the possession of power soon alters and vitiates their hearts, which are at the same time sure to have leavened and puffed up to an unnatural size, by the deceitful incense of false friends and by the prostrate submission of parasites. First they grow indifferent to all their good designs, then drop them. Next, they lose their moderation. Afterwards, they renounce all measures with their old acquaintances and old principles, and seeing themselves in magnifying glasses, grow in conceit, a different species from their fellow subjects. And so, by too sudden degrees become insolent, rapacious and tyrannical, ready to catch all means, often the vilest and most oppressive, to raise their fortunes as high as imaginary greatness. So that the only way to put them in mind of their former condition, and consequently of the condition of other people, is often to reduce them to it, and to let others of equal capacities share the power in their turn. This also is the only way to qualify men, and make them equally fit for domination and subjection. A rotation therefore, in power and magistracy, is essentially necessary to a free government."[3]

Many of the Founding Fathers embraced the principle of rotation in office. The Pennsylvania Constitution of 1776, the most radical constitution of the revolutionary era, imposed a strict four-year limit on the legislature. In 1776, Thomas Jefferson proposed a resolution in the Continental Congress saying that "to prevent every danger which might arise to American freedom by continuing too long in office," members of Congress should serve no more than two years. His proposal was rejected, but a modified version calling for only three years in office won approval in 1777.[4] Ten of the thirteen new states limited their governors to a one-year term, while New York and Delaware allowed a three-year term. The revolutionaries believed that such limits would ensure that officeholders reflect the makeup and outlook of the citizens they claimed to represent.

Perhaps understandably, the first attempt to enforce the term limits met with resistance from the incumbent delegates. When two delegates from Rhode Island were asked to retire at the end of their three years, they refused. The delegates fought "tooth and toenail to retain their seats," James Monroe, a future president, recalled. "I never saw more indecent conduct in any Assembly before." Fearing the controversy would prevent Congress from finishing its work in time, the members reluctantly dropped the issue and the delegates from Rhode Island stayed on. The first attempt to limit terms of office in America had failed.[5]

When the Constitution was debated in 1787, the sour experience with term limits in the Continental Congress convinced many delegates not to include them in the new founding document. But the delegates were decidedly in favor of a turnover of legislators. Roger Sherman of Rhode Island spoke for many delegates when he commented that Congress should be made up of "citizen legislators" who through rotation in office would "return home and mix with the people. By remaining at the seat of government, they would acquire the habits of the place, which might differ from those of their constituents."[6]

One reason why Jefferson originally wanted to oppose the Constitution was that it didn't include a term limit. "The second feature I dislike, and strongly dislike, is the abandonment, in ever instance, of the principle of rotation in office," Jefferson wrote in a letter to James Madison.[7] But while mandatory term limits were not part of the new Constitution, many delegates assumed that voluntary term limits would be the norm. It never even occurred that serving in Congress would become a career. In the first House election after George Washington was elected president, 40 percent of incumbents were defeated, laying to rest many fears of an entrenched "government of strangers."[8]

Up until the Civil War an average of 80 percent of incumbents who sought reelection won, but the tradition was for members to serve only four years in the House and six in the Senate. In a typical election a third of incumbents would retire so that the total turnover was 40 to 50 percent of Congress.[9] President Andrew Jackson spoke for the prevailing consensus in favor of term limits when he wrote in 1829 that "No man has an intrinsic right to an official post . . . rotation would have healthful action to the system of government." His advice was generally followed. During the nineteenth century the average member served only 4.5 years in office.

Abraham Lincoln, for example, had a personal informal rotation agreement with his political rivals. He served a single term in the House in the 1840s and then moved back to Illinois, not to return to Washington until he was elected president. Lincoln was a firm supporter of rotation in office. He once wrote, "If our American society and United States Government are overthrown, it will come from the voracious desire for office, the wriggle to live without toil, work and labor—from which I am not free myself."[10]

Political scientist Charles Kesler has written that the practice of rotation, under which incumbent legislators were denied renomination after serving one, two, or three terms, was a sign of keen competition and circulation of talent. He noted that "the parties and the country enjoyed the best of both worlds . . . a circulation of capable and experienced men through public office, with the possibility of keeping truly exceptional ones in office if circumstances demanded it."[11]

The conduct of the House's business also discouraged extended tenure in office. The House leadership was not driven by seniority, and party control frequently shifted. House members who wanted a career in politics were compelled to run for the Senate, seek a position in the executive branch, or return home and run for governor. Of the seven Speakers of the House elected between 1870 and 1894, for example, one was elected in his third term of service, two in their fourth, two in their fifth, one in his sixth, and one in his seventh.[12] In 1811, Henry Clay was elected Speaker of the House at the start of his *first* term! Contrast that with Jim Wright, elected Speaker in 1987 in his seventeenth term, or Thomas Foley, elected in 1989 in his thirteenth term.

House seniority began to rise after the turmoil of the Civil War and the establishment of the seniority system. By the turn of the century the number of members who retired before each election was down to 15 percent. Between 1860 and 1920, the average length of service doubled from four to eight years. In 1901, when the 57th Congress convened, for the first time less than 30 percent of members were freshmen. In 1981, when the 97th Congress convened, 17 percent were newly elected. In 1989, when the 101st Congress convened, less than 8 percent were newly elected.[13]

Another major change in Congress since the nineteenth century concerns the amount of time it is in session. Even forty years ago, Congress would meet for two months a year—and meeting for three months was considered unusual. A congressman was more or less compelled to be a citizen-legislator; he would go home after a session and spend most of his time running a business, practicing law, or whatever. Today, the sheer size and scope of the federal government has made service in Congress a full-time job, and most who are elected have to give up their careers. But with each passing year of congressional service, members are more reluctant to go back home and reenter the job market. In 1989 ethics legislation actually banned members of the U.S. House from practicing many professions and severely limited their power to earn any outside income. This encouraged even more members to consider Congress their "career" and forsake any thought of ever returning to private life.

The first popular movement for term limits came in the 1940s, after President Franklin Roosevelt broke the two-term tradition started by George Washington. The Twenty-second Amendment was introduced in 1947 by the new majority of Republicans in Congress. But despite its partisan origins, a great many Democrats agreed that violation of the two-term tradition for president made its codification necessary. Today, that same thinking motivates supporters of legislative term limits.

The amendment was ratified in 1951, with seven Democratic-controlled states providing the final necessary votes. The *Washington Post* editorialized that "power-grasping officials are common enough in history and current world experience to warrant this safeguard."[14]

Members of Congress were nevertheless horrified at the mere suggestion that the principle of term limits extend to them. During the 1947 debate on the Twenty-second Amendment, Sen. W. Lee O'Daniel (D.-Texas) offered an amendment to limit the terms of all federal officials. His proposal was rejected by a vote of 82 to 1, with O'Daniel's the only vote in favor.[15] In the 1950s, both Presidents Truman and Eisenhower endorsed a twelve-year limit on terms for congressmen and senators. But the proposal got nowhere—until the late 1980s, when the excesses of Congress roused voters to action.

Ironically, Congress has required that the Pentagon's Joint Chiefs of Staff be limited in their service. Col. John Peale, head of personnel at the Joint Staff, says the military has found that generals take up to six months to master their duties on the Joint Staff. Then they spend a year making valuable contributions, followed by a year or so during which they typically slow down and rest on their laurels. Peale believes that at some point between two and three years more fresh blood is needed.[16]

Today, examples of working term limits proliferate. The governors of twenty-five states are limited to two terms, while the governors and all statewide officials in Virginia, New Mexico, and Kentucky are limited to a single four-year term. One study found that states with such term limits tended to have much more political competition for governor.[17]

Within Congress, attempts to revive the tradition of rotation in office for members of Congress surfaced rather early—in the late 1970s. Sens. William Armstrong (R.-Colo.) and Gordon Humphrey (R.-N.H.) both promised to retire after two terms, and, to everyone's surprise, did precisely that. For others the addiction of office proved too much. As first-time candidates Sens. Dennis DeConcini (D.-Ariz.), Malcolm Wallop (R.-Wyo.), and Nancy Landon Kassebaum (R.-Kansas) all pledged to serve only twelve years in office. All are now in their third terms. In 1988, DeConcini was running for his third term on the dubious claim that he could better fight for a twelve-year limitation if he were in the Senate for eighteen years. Kassebaum announced her candidacy for a third term in 1989 by saying that she was convinced her seniority "could be put to good and worthwhile purposes."[18]

The only limits on political office that will work today are those that are mandatory.

# 10

---

# ANSWERING OBJECTIONS TO TERM LIMITS

---

*Any reform as sweeping as term limitation is going to be contro-versial. Term limits opponents raise a variety of objections. They claim it will limit choice at the polls, cost the people the service of experienced legislators, and enhance the power of staffs and lobbyists—among other arguments. These are legitimate ques-tions and they deserve full answers. Here are the most common objections to term limits and some substantive responses:*

*The high 1992 turnover in Congress makes term limits unnecessary. The results of the 1992 primaries show that incumbents can be beaten.*

No argument against congressional term limits is more ironic than that the high turnover on Capitol Hill in a single election year renders the whole idea of term limits moot.

The reality is that without term limits there will be the wrong kind of turnover, for the wrong reasons, and with the wrong results.

Almost all the turnover in 1992 is due to three simple (and simply outrageous) reasons: redistricting, the House Bank scandal, and this year's once-in-a-lifetime campaign fund "re-tirement bonus." How often can voters count on such a politi-cal windfall?

Redistricting comes once every decade, and the voters hardly have a say in deciding who stays and who goes. That is determined by the census and state legislatures, which frequently punish a few incumbents of the opposite party while protecting all their friends.

The 1992 "retirement bonus," which allows members elected before 1980 to keep all their campaign funds for personal use if they leave office before January 1, 1993, is, thankfully, a one-time affair, and far too high a price to pay for sending old bulls to pasture on a regular basis.

That leaves the prospect of relying on some kind of scandal every two years to clean House. Cynics suggest that voters can count on the exposure of some sort of chicanery or corruption every few months, but is that really the best viable system for creating open seats?

Even if we could depend on sixty or seventy forced, bribed, or redistricted retirements every two years, it still isn't the right kind of turnover. Most elections would still be uncompetitive. Local electorates have become politically comatose, drugged by decades of propaganda, free mail, and pork.

Most congressional retirements are also usually announced at the last minute, just before the filing deadline. That gives His Incumbency's faithful administrative assistant a leg up on the opposition. He is ready with the contacts, the mailing lists, and the money needed to get elected. He's likely been in Washington so long that he thinks everyone shops at the Gourmet Safeway in Georgetown, roots for the Redskins, and watches C-SPAN at night.

To prepare for his election, a typical congressional aide will rent a condominium in the largest city in the district, swap his D.C license plates for new ones from back "home," and hire a coach to teach him how to talk like the "folks" he grew up with. Then, when he's elected, three-quarters of His Incumbency's old staff will just get shuffled around—with a pay raise, of course. That isn't turnover, it's reheating the leftovers.

But the real problem isn't turnover in the first place. The problem is what happens to members after they've stayed in office for a decade or more. The real problem is not lack of new faces. It's that when members have been in office too long, the minds behind the faces start thinking the same way—they all want to turn into career politicians, concerned mostly about themselves, their power, and their perks.

So all the ballyhoo about the turnover of 1992 will ultimately give us nothing but a bunch of new faces that, in a few years, will probably be like all the others. Watch closely as this transformation occurs. It's not really their fault. They can't help it.

Should they receive disability payments or workmen's compensation for this sinister disease? Perhaps, as term limits supporters understand, an ounce of political prevention will do it. Rx: Term limits. Take one every six years.

*Term limits will restrict the choice of voters at the ballot box. They are undemocratic.*

If a majority of people supports term limits as a condition of employment for their elected officials, then term limits *are* democracy in action. They will merely be added to existing restrictions such as age and length of residency.

This argument, of course, also implies that voters now have a choice. Currently, the reelection rate for incumbents is above 95 percent for both Congress and most state legislatures. Because a challenger has little chance of raising enough money to compete effectively—to become known—few voters will vote for him, for they are understandably unwilling to cast a ballot for someone they know almost nothing about. As a result, rather than vote for an incumbent they don't like, over half the people don't vote at all.

The vast majority of the American people believe the only way they can ensure a real choice at the ballot box is to guarantee, democratically, that *no one* have a lifetime hold on an office. Limiting terms will also create opportunities for "new faces," and people such as women and minorities who at present can't compete for seats on an equal footing.

Term limits can be compared to some forms of environmental regulation. Dwight Lee, professor of economics at the University of Georgia, says term limits resemble restrictions placed on pollution. Opponents of pollution-control legislation could argue that the American people are able to reduce pollution by selecting products that are environmentally sound and rejecting those that are not. In theory, consumers are able to learn enough to be able to buy and select only those products that cause the least pollution. But they have powerful incentives not to: the polluting products may cost less and appeal more to the senses.

A similar situation can be found in politics. Voters heartily disapprove of the work of Congress as a whole, yet most vote to reelect their own congressman. He or she at least provides attractive goodies and valuable constituent services. Term limits are a form of "fiscal pollution control" that contain the amount of damage voters can inflict on the country as a whole by voting their own self-interest locally. They are an agreement by which voters give up their own esteemed representative in Washington in order to remove members from other districts or states whose collective behavior so disturbs them.

*Term limits will force valuable and experienced legislators out of office.*

Quite the opposite. Term limits will open up offices and let many capable people move in. People exist who do not want to make a career out of politics but would be willing to serve for a few years if they thought they could actually change policy. Under current conditions, they have little chance of influencing public policy unless they commit to a political career. They would have to outlast the current leadership of Congress and the committee chairmen in order to gain the seniority necessary to affect policy. If terms were limited, talented people, sure of policy influence in a few years, would be encouraged to run for office.

Many of the longtime incumbents they would replace, moreover, clearly suffer from "burnout." But they enjoy the power, prestige, perks, pensions, not to mention income, of politics. "I know a lot of members who have exhausted their intellectual capacities and are just hanging on because they have nothing else to do," says Rep. Bill McCollum of Florida.[1]

Rep. Andy Jacobs of Indiana, a supporter of term limits, reports that many members would welcome the chance to take a "sabbatical" from Congress if they knew their old seat would come vacant again in a few years.[2]

And, of course, term limits can still allow for long political careers. They just require that officeholders seek promotion up the political ladder. And the best ones will. Capable local government officials can run for state assembly, assembly members can seek state senate seats, and state legislators might think about running for Congress. Many statewide offices that seldom open up unless someone dies or retires would become available to capable people. Truly worthwhile legislators would have somewhere to go.

History is full of examples of prominent legislators who served long careers without staying in any one office forever. Henry Clay served seven terms in the House of Representatives, but only two of them were consecutive. Sen. Bill Armstrong of Colorado served in public life continuously from 1962 to 1991, but he never served in one office for more than twelve years. Former members of Congress would also be available to serve in the executive branch, industry, judiciary, and think tanks.

*We need people who are masters in the art of governing. A large rookie class of legislators would be largely ignorant of public policy issues.*

This argument ignores the fact that we somehow manage with a new president and executive branch officials every four or eight years. Why couldn't Congress function with a hundred new members every two years? Today, it takes an average of nineteen years to become chairman of a committee in the House. Does anyone really believe it takes that long to master a specialty?

James Spainhower, former Democratic state treasurer and state legislator from Missouri, scoffs at the suggestion that public office is something beyond the ability of most people to master: "I don't think any job in representative government is so difficult and complicated that an intelligent, committed person can't get on top of it within a year or so." He also points out that if a legislator is neither intelligent nor committed he can stay in office for twenty years and never be effective.[3]

As for our current members being highly knowledgeable, there is often "no there there." Members of Congress appear well informed only because they have aides who ply them with speech cards and talking points. If they had to rely on their own wits, a good many congressional "experts" would flounder.

Consider what happened in 1986 when then-Democratic Rep. Mike Barnes, a subcommittee chairman on the House Foreign Affairs Committee, was suddenly given a pop quiz on foreign policy issues during the taping of a Baltimore TV show. He was unable to name the leader of the African National Congress—Nelson Mandela—even though he was a leading backer of sanctions against South Africa. "The name slips my tongue," the bewildered Barnes admitted. Nor could he name the current prime minister of Israel.

Sen. Barbara Mikulski, then a Democratic House member, thought the leader of the ANC was Jonas Savimbi, the head of the anticommunist UNITA rebels in Angola. She looked pained when she couldn't think of the new Israeli prime minister. "Can we turn this thing off?" she asked the TV interviewer nervously. Wendy Sherman, Mikulski's campaign manager, attacked the TV station for conducting "board game politics" and said Representative Mikulski had been caught in an "unexpected moment."

Rep. Guy Vander Jagt of Michigan wasn't so sure. He said most lawmakers "would get about the same grade they did" on such a quiz.

*The problems America faces today require experienced, professional legislators.*

Perhaps the opposite is true. After all, what has all the "experience" of our professional legislators done for us lately? Some would say that our nation's problems may be so systemic and our current lawmakers so involved in creating them, that what we really need is congressmen inexperienced in the ways of government—people who don't have a stake in existing programs and can thus radically reform them.

"Professionalism and careerism in politics is the bane of democratic governance. There is no empirical evidence that professional politicians do a better job of governing than amateurs at any level of government," reports Mark Petracca of the University of California.[4]

Our "experienced" legislators have failed effectively to reach budget decisions, improve transportation, provide decent education for our children, produce clean air, eliminate crime from our streets, or manage the bureaucracy. In one instance, our "professional" legislators actually believed that nothing would go wrong if they provided virtually unlimited federal deposit insurance to the nation's S&Ls and then allowed them to invest in everything from sperm banks for horses to windmill farms. S&L owners did the expected thing. They played their institutions as if they were chips on a roulette table at a casino. If the investment came up black they won, if it came up red the taxpayers lost. The gaming losses from this colossal governmental blunder will cost every American family of four about five thousand dollars.

Politicians—as opposed to citizen legislators—have experience in creating illusions and deceptions. "Professional" politicians lose touch with the real world. America needs people with skills in different walks of life, those who build businesses, practice medicine, and run volunteer agencies—not career legislators who may know the legislative rules or the old-boy network, but little else.

During the budget summit meetings preceding the disastrous 1990 budget agreement, in which President Bush broke his "no new taxes" pledge, Iowa Rep. Jim Lightfoot made some interesting calculations about the budget negotiators. He found that the eleven House members who negotiated the deal averaged 60.4 years of age. They included six lawyers, one minister, one college professor, and three with some prior business experience. The three businessmen had just over fourteen years of practical experience. The House summiteers had worked a total of 378 years in their careers, only forty-seven of which had been in private life. In other words, 87 percent of their experience had been in government jobs and elected office.

Lightfoot firmly believes the 1990 agreement was a disaster in part because of who designed it. "The players were the same people who pushed through Congress all the current programs that have gotten us into our current mess," Lightfoot concluded. "They were unwilling to admit they had been wrong so they merely applied a few band-aids and raised taxes."[5] Isn't it just possible that members with more practical experience in the real world and less in the arcane art of legislating would have done a better job?

The idea that only experienced people can make decisions is an elitist one that rejects the very premise of democracy: that ordinary people have extraordinary possibilities.

*Term limits will merely shift power away from elected officials to unelected staffers and lobbyists.*

"Term limits will mean that the institutional memory and

expertise of Congress will be lodged either in the permanent bureaucracy and/or the business/corporate lobbies. Those will be the only people who will have the information and resources to put that information to work. Everybody else will be an amateur," notes Ann Lewis, a leading Democratic political consultant.[6]

This is a highly blinkered view of how legislatures work. Gobs of information is available to lawmakers, only some of which comes from lobbyists and bureaucrats. A good legislator treats it as he would information in a library—you have to sort out the good from the bad.

It's hard to imagine how, right now, there could be any closer linkage between powerful special interests and the current leadership of Congress and a host of state legislatures. Since many career legislators have no business or profession to which to return, they depend heavily on special interests for both information and support, and as a result are subservient to their demands. "The way Congress works today is depressing," says retiring Rep. Vin Weber. "Members tell the public when they campaign that they favor, say, the environment. They then turn right around and tell a special interest group that they'll protect them by getting a special exemption or regulation written for them. In theory, the elected officials are supposed to represent their constituents. But in reality, it's a special interest game."[7]

Legislators at the state level are no less beholden to special interests. In 1990, when the California legislature held hearings on a term limit initiative, Assemblyman Tom Bane argued with its sponsor, Pete Schabarum, that term limits would "turn this legislature over to big power special interests." Schabarum, then a Los Angeles County supervisor and a former three-term state legislator, shot back: "Special interests already run this legislature. Can I make that any clearer?"[8]

The explosion in the number of lobbyists and staffers occurred alongside that of career-oriented, lifetime-tenured legislatures. Careerism breeds reliance on staff—senior members, who have struggled to bring more programs and projects under their jurisdiction, are those most dependent on staff and lobbyists, not the idealistic, hot-shot freshmen. New members start out like Jimmy Stewart in *Mr. Smith Goes to Washington*, ready to slay dragons. But after a few terms of mutual backscratching, most incumbents relax and enjoy their power: they read prepared speeches, ask prepared questions and sign prepared mail. The staff helps them.

The most powerful staffers work for committee chairmen, and their tenure is secure only so long as their boss or patron is reelected. The longer a member serves in office the more powerful his staff becomes. When a new chairman takes over a committee he invariably brings in many new people. Capitol Hill newspaper *Roll Call* notes that new chairmen frequently insist on picking their own teams, regardless of the quality of work of the existing aides. A limit on terms would end the era of entrenched committee chairmen and the powerful staffs they spawn. No wonder surveys of staff members by the Sindlinger Organization found that over 70 percent of them oppose term limits.

Most other staffers, including those in a member's personal office, perform administrative or clerical tasks and are subject to a great deal of turnover. The average tenure of personal staffers in the House is only 2.9 years, with 70 percent having five years or less of Hill experience. Senate staffers serve an average of 3.5 years, and 41 percent have been on the job for a year or less.[9]

Limits on staff could accompany term limits, as Proposition 140 in California proved. It curbed the "aides epidemic" in the legislature by reducing its budget by 38 percent.[10] Patty Quate, who worked for one of the few California legislators who favored term limits, opposed them herself because they meant "job insecurity." She didn't know a single staffer in the State Capitol who favored the 1990 initiative.[11]

Critics also say that term limits might increase influence peddling by putting pressure on members of Congress to curry favor with those that might reward them with future employment. But few members are likely to become lobbyists, because the turnover would quickly make their contacts obsolete and their influence limited.

If special interests and legislative staffs believe term limits would indeed enhance their power, they don't act that way. In California, lobbyists gave over $3 million to defeat term limits last year. They gave almost no money to proponents of the measures. Interest groups benefit from longstanding relationships with legislators. Fred Eckert, who served in the New York state senate from 1974 to 1982, noted that "Lobbyists spend a lot of time educating members in their issue and how important their industry is. They certainly don't want to lose that investment."[12] Special interests would go broke trying to buy off Congress if terms were limited.

*By removing experienced members, term limits would increase the power of the permanent bureaucracy.*

Washington is a city of relationships. Members of Congress don't vote for abstract programs. They vote for budget items that have been pressed upon them by lobbyists, friends, colleagues, experts, and the media. Congressional hearings are dominated by three groups: government employees, people from private organizations who receive government grants, and consultants paid by the government to monitor programs. Few if any witnesses argue against the bureaucrats and their programs.

Political analyst James Payne found that the most senior congressmen are the least willing to question the premises of bureaucrats. What happens in Congress resembles the sort of brainwashing that went on during the Korean War, in which American POWs were persuaded to believe the most outlandish things. The longer members of Congress are exposed to the propaganda and beseechings of bureaucrats the greater their advocacy of the programs and the less the skepticism needed to be adequate watchdogs of the public purse.[13]

"When new people are elected to Congress, both they and the new staffers they bring with them start with a fresh perspective," affirms former Rep. Hal Daub of Nebraska, present director of government affairs for Deloitte and Touche, an accounting firm. "Term limits will actually help control bureaucrats. They are a good way to reestablish an adversarial attitude towards the bureaucracy."[14]

Just as special interests set their sights on legislators, so too does the bureaucracy. The longer a legislator is around, the greater the risk of a cozy relationship. Independent shorttimers will be much more likely to discipline the bureaucracy than to be absorbed by it.

*Those serving in a term-limited Congress would be less devoted to the issues and more concerned with money and politics.*

Think about it: If potential candidates for office know at the outset that they cannot make a career of legislative service, they will be motivated more by issues and service than by personal political power or financial gain. There will always be those who abuse power and position. But term limitation is the one reform that will reduce it to a minimum. It will automatically cleanse the system of such people.

*Elected officials need time to accomplish their plans and policy goals, something they wouldn't have if their service were limited.*

The argument can be made that term limits will lengthen rather than shorten the time horizons of lawmakers. Today, legislators often think ahead only as far as the next election. Those who view public office as a lifetime career can always find excuses not to take the electoral risk of pursuing difficult policy goals.

With a fixed number of terms, on the other hand, officeholders will have to move quickly to achieve their goals. As leadership changes with each session of Congress or the legislature, entrenched leadership, which now frustrates the goals of many thoughtful legislators, will be a thing of the past. The seniority system will be scrapped, and the resulting changes may break the kind of logjam that often makes legislative committees handling tort reform and criminal justice issues a graveyard for many needed reforms.

A term limit on legislators might be viewed the same way a football team views the limited amount of time it has to score points. It will spur them to get the job done before the whistle ends the game.

*Public financing of campaigns, or restrictions on campaign contributions and spending, are better reforms.*

The only effective way to level the political playing field is to limit terms. Spending limits simply enhance the existing advantages of incumbency. Challengers, to have any chance of winning, must raise and spend more than incumbents who, in reality, spend public money for the weapons of victory: staff, publicity, newsletters, travel, pork-barrel projects.

Public financing of campaigns is also flawed. Not only would it do nothing to offset the advantages of incumbency, it could lead to a colossal waste of taxpayers' money. Consider the case of Lenora Fulani, the candidate of the Marxist and antisemitic New Alliance party. Although her party was denounced as a "cult" by its 1984 presidential candidate, Fulani has received over $1 million in federal matching funds in her 1992 race for president. Public financing would also fund less bizarre candidates, who also had no chance of winning, with money the taxpayers would be unwilling to give voluntarily. Thomas Jefferson once wrote, "To compel a man to furnish contributions of money for the propagation of opinions he disbelieves is sinful and tyrannical."

Among all the proposed reforms to clean up American

politics, only term limitation drives right at the heart of the problem: breaking up the "ruling class" mentality that accompanies lifetime tenure in office.

But supporters of the above reforms also have a reason to push for term limits, despite their doubts. Any attempt to take away the advantages of incumbents would have to be passed by a Congress made up of the current incumbents. None of their solutions has a ghost of a chance unless politicians are threatened with the prospect of term limits. Try to think of a group of incumbents that has passed a campaign finance reform benefiting challengers more than incumbents. There isn't one. Incumbents won't pass such reforms—it's like asking chickens to deliver themselves to Colonel Sanders.

But there is one way to get some desirable reforms passed. Policemen don't always have to shoot a suspect to apprehend him. Sometimes they have only to take their guns out and point them at the suspect.

The threat of a limit on congressional service might be just the weapon necessary to generate real campaign reform. Members who are barred from making Congress a lifetime career might drum up the courage to enact legislation sunsetting government agencies and saying no to pork-barrel spending. They might go beyond the cosmetic perk cleaning that House Speaker Tom Foley conducted in the spring of 1990 and really do away with all the unessential privileges and perks of office.


Imagine Congress as a pirate ship. As pirates go, congressional pirates are a friendly lot, the kind that joke as they relieve you of your valuables. They never *really* hurt anyone, but for decades their pirate ship has been preying on the taxpayers, slipping into port in the dead of night to pick the pockets of sleeping citizens with stealthy tax increases. Its regulatory cannon have intimidated countless businessmen and its mandates have led many a local official to lose sleep wondering how to pay for them. Sometimes the pirates curry favor with the inhabitants of some towns that impress them, but they are fickle and snatch back their gifts at the slightest hint of disrespect. On the whole, the crew of the pirate ship *Congress* is arrogant. They even demand that the citizens they plunder subsidize propaganda promoting the exploits of those who spend it.

After many years of this, the citizens have had enough. They decide to build a sleek, modern Coast Guard cutter to pursue the congressional pirate ship. They base its construction on some ideas left by honored patriots who lived many generations ago. They christen it the *Term Cutter*, and dispatch it to catch the lumbering pirate ship with its congressional crew.

Now, the pirate ship *Congress* is well armed and huge. But in its long voyages between ports of call it has picked up barnacles that haven't been scraped off in years, slowing the ship's progress. Its crew has not had to fight a competitive contest in years, and some of the men are slow and out of training. The ship itself has not been cleaned in years, and many skeletons are stored in its closets, while parasites called "lobbyists" cling to its hull.

The congressional pirates spy the Coast Guard cutter on the horizon, but at first they ignore it. They are confident they can outrun it, just as they have outrun all previous pursuit vessels the voters on shore have launched. But this time they are wrong. The *Term Cutter* makes a surprisingly swift adversary and begins gaining on the *Congress*. Soon it will be within range and able to fire its sophisticated weaponry. The crew of the *Congress* begins to worry. They fire cannon loads of press releases at the pursuing ship, but to no avail. They offer to buy out the crew with some choice scraps from the congressional pork barrel, but they are spurned.

The crew of the *Congress* now starts to panic. Their old

weaponry may not be a match for their term limits pursuer. They can only be assured of escape if they can pick up speed and outrun it, so they begin scouring the decks for items to throw overboard to lighten their load. The first thing over the side is an ancient skeleton called the House Bank. That is followed by parking tickets that have been fixed, free prescription drugs they have collected, and a bit of franked mail. Their speed picks up, but not nearly enough to outrun the *Term Cutter*.

They case about for other things to throw overboard, but there is resistance. When a large safe marked "Pay Raise" is dragged up on deck, many members threaten to mutiny if it is tossed overboard. Meanwhile, the tension on board continues to rise as the *Term Cutter* pulls ever closer. Finally, the crew begins to discuss the possibility of giving up their life of piracy and engaging in open and honest commerce. The vote is hurriedly taken . . .

The point of this fantasy is to note that nothing prevents the existing incumbents in Congress from slowing down the term limits bandwagon. All they have to do is follow filmmaker Spike Lee's advice and Do the Right Thing. Make tough choices. Deliver efficient services. Avoid recurrent tax increases. Draw distinctions between essential and optional programs.

By becoming the kind of leaders that once again uphold voters' interests and values, members of Congress can restore the trust of the people. But there is precious little evidence that they will do so unless pressured.

*Term limits will tilt the balance of power from Congress to the president.*

When Congress passed the Twenty-second Amendment in 1951 limiting the president to two terms, it made the legislative branch more powerful, giving it more control over the bureaucracy. Most bureaucrats jump to attention when members of Congress call. After all, they are likely to remain in office long after a president and his appointees have left town.

But the Founding Fathers envisioned Congress as a representative body, not the entrenched micromanaging monster it has become. Its job is to make policy, not implement it. Considerable experience in government isn't necessary for that; considerable experience in life is. As Terry Considine, the father of term limits in Colorado, puts it: "We'd have a better Congress if more of them would remember their job is to write the music, not direct the orchestra."[15]

Over the last forty years, Congress has increasingly usurped the authority of the executive branch and grown more arrogant. As evidence, see the many laws from which it has exempted itself. James Madison warned against such attitudes in Federalist 57: "If this spirit shall ever be so far debased as to tolerate a law not obligatory on the Legislature as well as on the people, the people will be prepared to tolerate anything but liberty."

Congress and the president are coequal powers under the Constitution. If the terms of one are limited, the terms of the other should also be.

*Term limits will be harmful to minorities.*

California Assembly Speaker Willie Brown claimed during the debate over Proposition 140 that term limits would be particularly damaging to minorities because they need long-tenured incumbents with seniority to compete with the majority.

There is little evidence, however, that minorities have bought that argument. About 60 percent of blacks and Hispanics did oppose Proposition 140 after Speaker Brown flooded their neighborhoods with slate cards advocating a straight Democratic ticket and opposition to term limits. But term limits have carried a majority of the minority vote in most places where they've been on the ballot. The city of San Antonio, which has a 66 percent Hispanic population, gave term limits a 2 to 1 victory in May 1991.

The term limits battle in New Orleans pitted entrenched city council members against black voters who felt their real concerns were being ignored by an arrogant political machine. Incumbent black city council members ran radio ads declaring that term limits were racist and would deprive the community of "experienced leadership." But their arguments fell flat after the local Congress of Racial Equality endorsed the idea. "No one—black or white—has the right to unlimited time in office," George Ethel Warren, a black community activist since 1942, stated. "As soon as politicians get elected, they pass out enough favors so they can never be beaten." This view was clearly the more popular. New Orleans is 64 percent black, and the measure carried in almost every neighborhood.[16]

Kansas City saw another confrontation between a black political machine and minority voters in November 1990. The minority areas of Kansas City were dominated by Freedom, Inc., which began as part of the civil-rights movement in the 1960s but became a political machine dependent on government patronage jobs and sweetheart public contracts.

Henry Lyons, a black businessman, decided to challenge Freedom, Inc.'s domination of certain city council seats with a term limit measure. It was truly draconian: nine of the thirteen council members would have to leave office at the next election. Yet he won 57 percent of the vote citywide and nearly carried the minority areas.

Councilmen Charles Hazley and Robert Hernandez immediately filed suit in federal court charging that under term limits only "safe" minorities who wouldn't challenge the status quo would get elected. They claimed that while "they are not indispensable to their constituents, their experience is." Lyons's attorney, Terry Brady, responded that term limits allow voters to elect other qualified minorities or to elect a city council incumbent to another office.

Federal Judge Howard F. Sachs ruled that while he thought term limits were bad publicity policy, they violated neither the Constitution nor the Voting Rights Act. In court, Brady asked Hazley, a five-term councilman, if Henry Lyons, the sponsor of term limits, was black. "To the best of my knowledge," Hazley replied. Mr. Hernandez answered by saying there was "some question" about Lyons's race. After a pause, he added, "He's black, he's black. I'm just angry and nervous."

Although Hazley admitted that term limits were "race neutral," he argued that in practice they discriminated. He went on to say that the campaign for term limits had been racially motivated, but could provide no evidence. Indeed, he admitted that Freedom, Inc. had circulated flyers calling term limits "a racist, bossist, plantation-style effort to destroy our community."[17]

Despite such tactics, term limits won 44 percent of the vote in black areas. (Nationwide, polls show term limits are favored by blacks more than whites.)

Lyons says that far from being racist, term limits will allow "other voices in the minority community to be heard." In some cases, term limits could even mean more minority representation, since white incumbents often hold onto districts that have changed demographically simply because of their incumbent advantages.

*Lame duck congressmen would be less attentive to their constituents and more likely to vote against their wishes since they wouldn't have to face voters again.*

A study by economist John Lott in the journal *Public Choice* found that politicians in their last terms do not ignore citizens. Though their attendance record may decline slightly, they continue to vote as they always have. In addition, a member of Congress who is about to "go home" while still in the prime of life, and will have to live under the laws he or she has passed, will be more likely to think like his constituents.

Joe Clarke, a twenty-one-year veteran of Kentucky's house of representatives, says he has spent years trying to convince retiring legislators to vote his way and against the views of their districts—and routinely failed. He recounts that he reminded a lame-duck legislator that he did not have to worry about angry constituents if he voted against their interests because he wouldn't be on the ballot again. "No," the legislator told him, "but I'm going to be living back there."

*The seniority system in Congress would be severely damaged by term limits. Many states would lose valuable clout in Congress.*

The real power in Congress comes from chairing a committee, almost always a prize given to the most senior member on that panel. Far from being useful, this congressional "senility" system is a major obstacle to reform. That's why four House Democrats, led by Oklahoma Rep. David McCurdy, who oppose term limits recently suggested term limits for committee chairmen. Under their proposal, no one could chair a panel for more than eight years.

"Some committee chairmen are more feared than the House leadership," McCurdy declares. "Our intent is to reduce the possible arrogance that comes from having no accountability."[18] His fellow heretic, Rep. Dan Glickman of Kansas, says chairmen lose touch with the country because they "take on an aura of power that isolates them from what's happening."[19]

In 1981, the year Ronald Reagan became president, three House members became chairmen of key committees: Dan Rostenkowski became chairman of Ways and Means, Kika de la Garza of Agriculture, and John Dingell of Energy and Commerce. Since then they have held a hammerlock on the public policy issues under their jurisdiction.

Mr. Dingell, often called the House's "Chairmonster," employs bully-boy tactics so as constantly to expand the authority of his committee. His army of two hundred staffers is the most feared and out-of-control of the shock troops in Washington. Mr. Rostenkowski has blocked an important cut in the capital gains tax for years. And Mr. de la Garza has stymied any real reform of the nation's Soviet-style agricultural policies.

Each of these men secured his power largely by virtue of seniority, not merit. They had to serve an average of twenty-one years before their turn came at bat. Unsurprisingly, they and other chairmen are often more interested in protecting their hard-won turf than pushing through a substantive agenda.

Richard E. Cohen, author of a book on Congress called *Washington at Work*, says that having entrenched chairmen may have contributed to a ten-year stalemate in rewriting the Clean Air Act. Mr. Dingell and Rep. Henry Waxman, chairman of a key health subcommittee, are bitter adversaries and their feud helped kill sensible reform of the act throughout the entire Reagan presidency. Ronald Reagan is long gone from Washington, but the committee chairmen serve on, and on, and on.

Representative McCurdy points out that some committee chairmen already have term limits imposed on them. He himself chairs the Intelligence Committee and can serve a maximum of six years. The same rule applies to the House Budget Committee. But Mr. McCurdy concedes that the remaining chairmen are so powerful that he doesn't expect his proposal to pass any time soon. He says many of his colleagues have privately told him they like the idea, but "they're glad someone else is proposing it." Pretty clearly, the only way term limits will be imposed on committee chairmen is if they are imposed on all members.

A Congress purged of its most senior members would be able to select its leaders and committee chairmen on a rational basis, choosing those with talent and leadership qualities rather than those with the greatest staying power. There would be more competition for leadership posts and key committees.

Ideology would count more than loyalty to old bull legislators. And specific policy stands would affect leadership elections more than someone's ability to raise money on behalf of members.

*Term limits would do nothing to change Washington fundamentally. They would simply replace one set of politicians with another.*

With term limits, a different kind of person will seek office. Early evidence for this was shown by the people who filed to run for the first post-term limits legislation in California; there were many fewer lawyers and many more people with business and management experience. Whoever is elected under term limits will also face different incentives once in office.

Career-oriented legislators fall into a habit that is very dangerous in a government that claims to be "of the people." Longevity in government breeds a sense of ownership or proprietorship over government. Our Founding Fathers, on the other hand, envisioned elected officials who would serve as "trustees" and then retire. "In free governments, the rulers are the servants and the people their superiors and sovereigns," wrote Benjamin Franklin. "For the former therefore to return among the latter was not to degrade but to promote them." Compare that vision with the mindset of one longtime member of the California state legislature who criticized the FBI's investigation of bribery in the legislature: "This is my house. These are my friends." What he was saying was that he viewed the legislature as a private club for his gang and he resented having outsiders inquire into what went on behind their closed doors.

As many who have served in government have remarked, when someone starts talking about government as "us" rather than "them," it's time for them to leave. The problem today is that those who think of government as "us" can stay on and on. And they eventually become committee chairmen and legislative leaders. Those who want to buck the old-boy network and fight the special interests become frustrated and leave. One former congressman calls this Gresham's Law of Politics: bad legislators outlast and drive out good ones.

*Putting term limits on federal officeholders will put states that pass them at a disadvantage. They will lose seniority and clout.*

The damage done to individual states by an incumbent-entrenched Congress far outweighs the benefits of any pork-barrel projects members drag home. Many of the benefits that come to states from having senior members of Congress are an illusion, like an oasis in the desert that turns out to be an oil slick. Voters should demand of a member that he explain how his clout has made life in their state better for *most* people, not for just a select and favored few. The average senior member won't be able to do so.[20]

The campaign for term limits is also moving with a speed and degree of success that will probably force Congress to act on the issue in a few years. This year, fifteen states will have term limit initiatives on their ballot, representing over one-quarter of the nation's population. If voters in all or most of the twenty-two states that can have term limit initiatives on their ballots pass them, the political momentum may be irresistible.

*Term limits are a great idea, but they will never happen even if twenty-two states impose term limits on their own congressmen. The Supreme Court will invalidate them and the members of Congress will ignore the people's call for term limits.*

True, until recently, few political observers were willing to predict that term limits would win national acceptance, given the difficulty of passing a constitutional amendment. But after suitable pressure from voters, dozens of politicians began endorsing the concept, with varying degrees of sincerity. Now several legal scholars are convinced that the "Colorado" plan to have individual states limit the terms of their members of

Congress may be upheld as constitutional by the Supreme Court. The current Court strongly believes in federalism, and it may look favorably on states acting to correct what is a nationwide crisis in noncompetitive elections.

The term limitation movement has already been called the most important grass roots campaign of the 1990s. Its success has demonstrated the depth of the public's support and the political viability of the issue. Walter Dean Burham, a leading congressional scholar at the University of Texas at Austin, believes that "there really is a term limitation train leaving the station under a growing head of steam. There would seem to be a considerable chance—say 50-50 or so—that by the end of the decade, a constitutional amendment will be adopted to impose such a limitation at the federal level."[21]

Even some opponents of term limits, such as former House Majority Leader Tony Coelho, concede that they could apply to Congress and most state legislatures by the end of the decade. "Unless something drastic is done, term limits are going to sweep the country," he predicts. "Challengers will pledge support, incumbents will have to follow suit, and before you know it they could be called on their promise and term limits would be in the Constitution."[22]

Even if it does not ultimately succeed, the term limits movement will have served as a measure of the health of representative democracy and citizen politics in America. It is living proof that the people still want to control their own destiny.

# 11

---

# THE TERM LIMIT MOVEMENT

---

THE CONGRESSIONAL ELECTION of 1988 was a catastrophe because nothing happened. Only six House incumbents and one senator were defeated, the highest reelection rate in American history. Commentators nationwide decried this carbon-copy Congress and charged that its members had effectively built an impassable moat between themselves and their political competition. That's when many Americans woke up to the fact that they no longer controlled Congress.

The previous year, the stock market had suffered its worst crash since the Great Depression and people were just beginning to understand that the S&L bailouts were going to cost upwards of $400 billion. Taxpayers were nervous about the budget deficit, businessmen were worried about the trade deficit, and everyone was getting hysterical about the crack cocaine surplus.

Congress, in the meantime, seemed to be hibernating. It found time to celebrate its own bicentennial with a lavish party and train ride to New York commemorating its first session (with no incumbents) two centuries before; but it couldn't find time to pass budget and appropriation bills on schedule. It had been the same story in nine of the previous ten years.

The political strategy of the day was to propose a lot, pass a little, and blame everything on the White House—to shift

public attention away from Congress. Former Speaker Tip
O'Neill was enjoying his retirement, playing cards in Miami
Beach, and his successor, Jim Wright, was happy to let Michael
Dukakis take the spotlight in his presidential battle with Vice
President Bush that fall.

The press, as always, told everyone that presidential politics
was all that mattered, and that was fine with congressional
incumbents. If you're going to steal an election, best do it when
no one is watching.

Only six incumbents lost in the fall of 1988, the same number as in the previous election. Who needed to worry about the
voters anymore? Incumbency was not just an art for these
guys; they had winning elections down to a science.

The only problem had to do with the postelection scheme.
The script had been written months before, and no one knew
how, but the plot went awry that winter.

It wasn't supposed to be complicated. All they wanted was
more money. The decade of the 1980s had seen a lot of people
getting rich quick. It was time congressmen got theirs, too, but
they had to be patient for just a few more months.

First, they had to wait until everyone was reelected. Simply
follow the standard plan: spend millions of dollars on television ads to remind the voters about your friends, your clout,
and your connections; then let those steroid ads perform their
magic, and muscle your way to victory. Elections were the easy
part.

The hard part was the pay raise legislation. A small group of
senior members had been designated to devise the plan secretly. For months it was only whispered about, then, a few
days after the elections, everyone knew: it was time.

Word had spread among the members, like news of a pend-
ing escape from Alcatraz, that everything was "go": the tunnel
had been dug, the watches synchronized, the spoons filed into
daggers, the raft hidden down along the shore. Only a very few
knew exactly when the attempt would be made, but it was

some night soon, while the citizenry was asleep and the guards weren't looking.

Nothing was overlooked. A deal was struck between Republicans and Democrats that no one would squeal or use the pay raise vote in a future campaign. The White House made a similar agreement (ensuring that its own budget request would get speedy approval). Thus, no one in government would be watching, and the public would be too tired to care after the long presidential campaign.

Finally, everyone was given his or her script. The plan was elegant. Have a "commission" recommend the pay raise, tie it to a raise for the whole government, and have it go into effect automatically—without a separate vote and with President Reagan's lame-duck blessing. Most importantly, get the whole sordid mess done right after the elections, so the voters would have two whole years to forget about it. And in a final moment of inspired legislative legerdemain, have the whole proposal appended to an *ethics reform bill!*

But something went wrong. Some say it was the sudden economic downturn that winter, as real estate prices started to flatten out and people began to worry about the future. Others say it was just some sloppy staff work that let a few radio talk show hosts like Rush Limbaugh fire up the switchboards with angry populists.

A few old-timers still felt it was a matter of "no guts, no glory." Something like a 50 percent pay raise, secretly passed into law while no one was looking, required a Congress that could take some heat. But the temperature soon became unbearable, and several members began to flee the kitchen.

Speaker Wright himself finally caved and announced he would support the pay raise only if a private poll of Congress supported him. Knowing the list would be leaked to the media, no one signed up.

The pay raise was dead, at least for the time being. The big loser, of course, was Congress. The whole affair exposed the institution in the harshest possible light. To many voters, it seemed that the typical congressman was only concerned about his career, his pay raise, and his perks. Even worse, they felt that Congress was out of control. People began talking about limits. The Term Limits Movement was born.

For us, the picture started to come into focus that spring. A former congressman is always in demand to speak about Congress to audiences—a local church group, the monthly Rotary luncheon, and a seminar of government executives. Now, after each address, the same question came up: how do we put limits on Congress, clean the place up, and get back in control?

Each group offered the same answer: Term Limits.

Some early rumblings in favor of term limits had surfaced the year before. At the 1988 Republican Convention, former Rep. Tommy Harnett of South Carolina convinced delegates to write a pro-term limit plank into the platform. That fall, he penned a piece in support of term limits for the *Wall Street Journal*. He wrote, "It's time we told members that after a limited number of terms, we will give you a gold watch and send you home to live under the laws you passed while you were in Congress."[1]

The next year, in June 1989, the *Wall Street Journal* would become the first major newspaper in the country to support term limits editorially.


A few weeks after the congressional pay raise debacle, we had lunch in the Capitol with one of the most respected former congressmen, Walter Judd of Minnesota. (Judd was the co-founder of the Association of Former Members of Congress in 1970 along with the late Brooks Hays.) He was then almost ninety years old and had an incredible perspective on the political history of the twentieth century. He was a veteran of World War I, had been a surgeon at the Mayo Clinic, a medical missionary to China in the 1930s, and he was still giving lectures about the eleven presidents he had known. Elected to Congress in 1942, he had been a true citizen legislator, continuing his medical practice even after he was elected.

No one could possibly love Congress more than Walter Judd. But as we dined together in the Capitol Hill Club, you could almost see the pain in his heart. Congress was collapsing. Elections were becoming almost meaningless. Technology, television, ambition, and avarice were destroying Congress's humanity and its legitimacy.

Our discussion then turned to term limits. "It's the only solution," he agreed, "but Congress will never stand for it."

"You probably don't remember what happened in 1947," he surmised correctly. "Senator Lee O'Daniel tried to add congressional term limits to the language of the proposed Twenty-second Amendment limiting the president to two terms. He lost 82 to 1. His was the only affirmative vote."

But the national mood was different now. Congressional leaders on both sides of the aisle were admitting that Congress was becoming irrelevant—too big, too pompous, and too beholden to the God of fundraising. "They should change their titles," he declared. "They're not representatives. They're Delegates of Special Interests."

No one takes the time to be a legislator, "citizen" or otherwise. It's all PAC receptions, press conferences, and pettiness; 97 percent of the incumbents get reelected, yet 97 percent of the bills they propose never become law (and those that do result from grappling successfully with such issues as making April National Asparagus Month).

Walter Judd gave some modest encouragement: "Maybe Congress would listen to some of us, former members." We agreed to try.

The next week a letter went out asking for help from the six hundred former members whose addresses were available.

The response was encouraging. Hundreds wrote back, and most agreed that they were worried about Congress—the lack of competitive elections and the influence of money in politics.

Some, like Jerry Ford, Tip O'Neill, and Gene McCarthy, sent polite notes but declined. Others, like Jim Buckley, applauded our effort, but wouldn't join forces with us because of professional conflicts or an unwillingness to embarrass former colleagues.

One or two got downright nasty. The Honorable Frank M. Karsten wrote back the following:

> Dear Sir:
>
> For over two hundred years the people of the United States have been capable of deciding who they want to represent them in Congress and they certainly do not need any advice from a one-term-lightweight-Republican-Congressman like you.
>
> I am returning the junk you sent me and would suggest you use it for toilet paper.
>
> Frank M. Karsten[2]

Despite Karsten's eloquence in defense of himself and other career politicians, some of his former colleagues disagreed with him. A surprising thirty-three courageous former members were willing to stand up to the conventional wisdom and help establish a national group to campaign for term limits.

Some former members—or, as one of them describes himself, "reformed" members—were willing to take an active role. Donald M. Fraser, a former Democratic representative from Minnesota and now mayor of Minneapolis, agreed to cochair Americans to Limit Congressional Terms. Shortly thereafter, in February 1990, ALCT held its first press conference to announce a proposal for a constitutional amendment to limit terms. The campaign against the lifetime congressional career had been launched.

At the same time, local term limits organizations were

springing up in individual states across the country, resolutions were being introduced in state capitals, and petitions were being drafted to get initiative proposals to limit legislative tenure on the ballot in 1990.

By the end of February 1990, two state legislatures—South Dakota and Utah—had passed resolutions calling for a constitutional convention to consider limiting congressional terms. A few weeks later, activists at the state level started circulating petitions to gather the qualifying signatures for initiatives in Oklahoma, Colorado, and California.

In Oklahoma, independent businessman Lloyd Noble III won the race to get the first statewide vote on limiting tenure in office: On September 18, 1990, voters approved a twelve-year limit on state legislators by a margin of 67 percent to 33 percent. The measure carried all seventy-seven counties. It was endorsed by the incumbent governor, Republican Henry Bellmon, who said the measure would cure the problem of "electoral rigor mortis," because once incumbents gain seniority "they become powerful and are in a position to do favors for their own constituents."[3]

The measure was also backed by David Walters, the successful Democratic candidate for governor that fall. Term limits was a major theme in his upset primary win, and he went further by advocating a two-year ban on lobbying by legislators leaving office. "Take a trip down the hallways at the Capitol and count the former legislators who have become lobbyists. How do we know they weren't serving those same special interests while in the Legislature?" he asked.[4]

Colorado's term limit, the first in the nation to include a state's congressional delegation, was the brainchild of Terry Considine, a forty-four-year-old Republican state senator. Considine was first alerted to the state of politics in Colorado after a Republican gerrymander in 1981 curtailed the number of competitive races. By 1990, there had been twenty-four races for Congress under the new lines and only two changes of party. Not a single person in the state senate where Considine served had lost since 1982. In early 1990, Considine introduced a term limit bill in the legislature. It was promptly killed. Undeterred, he formed a group called Coloradans Back in Charge and gathered enough signatures to put his idea on the November 1990 ballot.

His proposal was opposed by organized labor *and* the Chamber of Commerce, both of which were comfortable with the status quo in the legislature. But Considine picked up some unusual support, including Herrick Roth, the reform-minded former head of the state's AFL-CIO, and the liberal *Denver Post*.

Considine then organized a grass roots lobby of four thousand volunteers to stump for the initiative, which carried easily with 71 percent of the vote. He promptly began organizing a nationwide term limit group called Americans Back in Charge to help other groups implement the "Colorado" plan by getting states to impose term limits on their federal representatives, thus making an end-run around the more cumbersome approach of calling for a constitutional convention.

Considine, who was principled enough to resign his state senate seat in early 1992 when he became a candidate for the U.S. Senate, says that the term limits movement is a revival of citizen activism similar to the wave of reform that brought the United States primaries, the right to vote on initiatives in twenty-two states, the direct election of senators, and votes for women. Each of those reforms was bitterly opposed by the political establishment of the day, yet each was eventually accepted. Considine views term limits as the beginning of a revival of citizen politics in America.


But the mother of all term limit battles was in California. Democratic Attorney General John Van de Kamp began circulating a term limit proposal in late 1989 to build support for his race for governor. But he coupled a twelve-year term limit on the legislature with a plan for publicly financing elections that would later prove highly unpopular.

This approach was unacceptable to a trio of citizen activists who were also pursuing a term limit initiative. Pete Schabarum, a Los Angeles county supervisor and former assemblyman, Mike Ford, a Marin County taxpayer activist, and Lewis Uhler, head of the National Tax Limitation Committee, placed a competing measure on the ballot. It was a much tougher measure in that it restricted all statewide officials, including the governor, to two four-year terms, the state senate to two terms, and the state assembly to three two-year terms. The measure also scrapped the lavish legislative pension system and imposed a 38 percent cut in the legislature's operating budget.

Both term limit proposals upset Assembly Speaker Willie Brown, a twenty-six-year legislative veteran and the most powerful politician in California. He disliked Proposition 131, the Van de Kamp initiative, but he was genuinely frightened by Proposition 140, the strict term limit. His fellow legislators were equally fearful. They shrank at the prospect of term limits as would Dracula at the sight of a cross. Only nine of the 120 state legislators wound up endorsing either term limit measure.

Willie Brown pressured or persuaded dozens of lobbyists and corporations to pony up $3 million for a sustained barrage of anti-term limits ads. State legislators contributed another $1.3 million. Brown then hired a consulting firm (aptly named BAD Campaigns) to come up with a series of scare tactics worthy of *Nightmare on Elm Street*. Brown was proud of what he and BAD Campaigns had pulled off in the past. After defeating a June 1990 initiative to ban gerrymandering in California, he boasted that his demagogic ads represented "the most extensive collection of con jobs I've ever seen."[5]

Mr. Brown and BAD Campaigns fashioned new con jobs for

the term limits battle. Their most popular one featured actress Angela Lansbury, who played a kindly crime-solver on the CBS series *Murder She Wrote*. She told viewers that if both term limits initiatives passed, "millions of your tax dollars will go to politicians' campaigns." But public financing was only part of Proposition 131, sponsored by John Van de Kamp, who lost the Democratic primary for governor. Proposition 140, the genuine term limits measure, had nothing to do with public financing. Mike Ford, a leader in the Proposition 140 campaign, dubbed the Lansbury ad "Distortions She Said."[6]

Another BAD Campaigns ad attacked "Proposition 140's true purpose—more power for special interests and greedy developers." Their mail warned that Prop 140 would lead to special interests dominating a legislature made up of "amateur politicians."[7] This assault fell flat with California voters, however; polls showed they believed 2 to 1 that most state legislators were already in hock to lobbyists. They also noted that the flood of special interest money was flowing to the people fighting term limits, not to its supporters.

Although the BAD Campaigns' barrage didn't destroy its target, its TV blitz onslaught badly lamed support for Prop 140, partly by lumping it in voters' minds with the less popular Proposition 131's public financing provisions. On election day, Proposition 131 lost almost every county, winning only 36 percent of the vote. Proposition 140, which had been leading by 2 to 1 in most polls, won with 52 percent of the vote. It carried most large counties, with the exception of Los Angeles and Willie Brown's San Francisco. While the vote may have been close, the victory in California was to the term limits movement what Bastille Day was to the French Revolution. Having won in the nation's largest state, term limits leaped onto the nation's political agenda.

The battle for term limits in California didn't end with the champagne toasts on election night. Prop 140's backers hoped that legislators would finally clean up their act now that the people had voted for a smaller, more responsive legislature. But, by and large, legislators flunked that test.

Indeed, the petulant reaction of many lawmakers to the curbs on their bureaucratic empire convinced many voters that in order properly to house clean, term limits would have to be joined by several other needed reforms.

Shortly after Proposition 140 passed, angry legislators filed suit in the California State Supreme Court challenging the proposition's constitutionality, and a contemptuous Assembly Speaker Willie Brown defiantly declared on national television that the court would invalidate the term limits. State Sen. Daniel Boatwright warned ominously that "Judges who rule on term limits should remember that if voters can limit legislators they can also limit the judiciary."[8]

Democratic Assemblyman Richard Floyd and other legislators became positively spiteful after the passage of term limits. Floyd virtually closed his district office and told constituents who voted for term limits to look for help elsewhere. His new office consisted of a part-time worker and an answering machine. "I'm depressed," he said. "There's no future for me. There's no future for my staff."[9] Indeed, there wasn't. Assemblyman Floyd was defeated for renomination in the June 1992 primary along with another longtime incumbent. Both had been placed in a largely black district through an impartial redistricting.

Assemblyman John Vasconcellos, a twenty-four-year incumbent best known for his eccentric advocacy of a "commission on self-esteem" in the 1970s, was even more bitter. He said he was thinking of resigning before his current term expired. "I'm reducing my working time to 40 hours a week from over 60," he told the *Los Angeles Times*. "I don't see any point in killing myself for people who apparently don't care if they have decent government or not." Mr. Vasconcellos said he couldn't believe the voters could be so "self-destructive" as to think that new blood in the legislature might be better than old.

In fact, some of that old blood left faster than term limits advocates had dared hope. Assemblyman Lloyd Connelly, a key committee chairman, retired to become a judge; and Mike Roos, the assembly speaker pro tem, resigned to head a group seeking to improve the public schools. Assemblyman Ted Lempert, a thirty-year-old political animal who had been elected in 1988, promptly announced he was running for Congress. Over 30 percent of the assembly members retired or ran for another office in 1992. The candidates running to replace them in office—for a maximum of six years—had generally more diverse backgrounds than the lawyers and legislative staffers that had dominated the legislature since the late 1970s.

Lewis Uhler, a coauthor of Proposition 140, applauded the incumbent exodus from the legislature. "In private life, if someone spends eight years in the same job, you wonder why he hasn't either been promoted or fired. Term limits mean the best legislators will try for promotion to Congress, statewide office or the non-profit sector. Anyone can still spend a lifetime in politics, but you must keep climbing the career ladder. The best ones will."[10]

Democrat Tom McEnery, a former San Jose mayor and friend of the embittered Assemblyman Vasconcellos, agreed. He says his friend "can make other contributions." He compares the legislature to a "hermetically sealed mayonnaise jar" which keeps members from realizing they are part of "a fatally flawed system."[11]

Ironically, for all their complaints that Proposition 140's budget cuts would emasculate the legislative staff and leave members awash in key issues, California's legislature wound up encouraging many of its best staffers to quit. To cushion the impact of the 40 percent cut in the legislature's budget, employees who agreed to quit were offered a generous five-month severance package and advantages in seeking civil service jobs. Instead of an expected 350 voluntary retirements, over 800 of the legislature's 2,800 employees left. "They ended up losing people they didn't want to lose," Assemblyman Tom McClintock reported.[12]

Many of the exiled staffers were bitter that their days in the state's corridors of power were over. When we visited the state capitol to address a legislative staffers association, we were startled at how the event had been advertised. A flyer, handed out at the door of the meeting, announced the talk would be entitled: "Why You Are Losing Your Jobs, And Why It's a Good Thing." The speaker was booed and hissed when he tried to defend term limits.

One of the most frequent complaints of departing staffers was that, in their absence, the legislature would be captured by lobbyists and have to depend on them for advice and information. But lobbyists didn't see it that way. They feared losing their "investments"—the longtime incumbents who have become attuned to their interests. Linda Muir, a lobbyist for the horse-racing industry, put her concerns succinctly: "An entire group of new members every six years, with no familiarity with the issue or the history of our industry, is very frightening. It scares the heck out of me."[13] The executive director of the California Commission on Aging said that many lobbies feared having to "educate" a whole new crop of legislators.[14]

Both lobbyists and legislators desperately tried to lock up the term limit ax before it could start swinging in 1996. The lawsuit filed by legislators claimed term limits were unconstitutional because they were undemocratic and would "reduce the legislature to an agency, rather than a co-equal branch of government."[15] Assembly Speaker Brown called them the equivalent of "terrorist bombs," and claimed they were racist since the most powerful minority politicians, like himself, were longtime incumbents.[16] That, of course, ignored the fact that legislative turnover would open up demographically changing districts to women and minorities.

The California Supreme Court ruled on the lawsuit against Proposition 140 in October 1991. In a 6 to 1 ruling it buried

most of the legal arguments against term limits. Declaring that
term limits were not undemocratic, it noted that the public
itself had voted to restrict service in the legislature. Installing
an electoral parking meter for legislators would encourage the
best ones to get on with the job and dispose of the worst before
they became entrenched. Efforts by the humiliated legislators
to have the U.S. Supreme Court reverse the California decision
failed in March 1992 when the nation's highest court refused
to hear their appeal.

Legislative term limits were now undeniably legal. The people had the right once again to take back control of their legislatures. The petty behavior of California's legislators in their
attempts to obstruct Proposition 140 will no doubt stick in
people's minds as further proof that too many politicians have
the imperial attitude that they are above oversight by the public. If term limits accomplish nothing else, they will tell elected
officials that they are the public's servants and not its masters.

Following the success of California's Proposition 140, many
states began gearing up to get their own initiatives on the ballot
in 1992 to take advantage of the heightened political participation that comes with a presidential election. Citizens in Washington State, however, decided not to wait, and began collecting
signatures in early 1991 to get the most ambitious term limitation proposal yet on the ballot that fall—Proposition 553.

This measure proposed to limit U.S. senators and representatives to twelve consecutive years in office, along with similar
limits on the governor, lieutenant governor, and state legislators. But there was one big difference: It was retroactive. Past
service would be counted: those members who had been in
office for twelve years when the measure became law would
have to leave at the end of their next term.

If Proposition 553 were approved on Election Day 1991, the
entire House delegation from Washington State, including
Speaker Tom Foley, would be out of office by 1994. These were
limits with teeth!

At first, polls showed overwhelming support for Proposition 553 and its backers were confident of victory.[17] But late in September, money started pouring into the state to stop Prop 553. The largest contributors against term limits were government employee unions, tobacco companies, such as Phillip Morris, and pressure groups, such as the National Rifle Association. Their principal argument was that the "draconian" term limits would leave Washington State at a disadvantage. Mindy Cameron of the *Seattle Times* described their tactics: "California was very much painted as the bogeyman. The thrust of the anti-term limit campaign was to say that if it passed, within three years we would lose all of our incumbents and, thus, our clout in Congress. California would then be free, willy-nilly, to drain the Columbia River, raise our power rates, and undermine our whole economy. . . . Some astute political observers bought into it."[18]

But opponents weren't satisfied that such a campaign would be enough. Rep. Al Swift became a point man against the initiative, even declaring his retirement from Congress in 1994 so he could "campaign against term limits without appearing to be self-serving." He certainly campaigned with a vengeance. In one radio debate, he warned that supporters of term limits are "so frustrated that they will voluntarily give up their rights. There is a parallel here with Nazi Germany, enormous frustration. . . . The Germans in the face of enormous inflation and enormous frustration voted to give away rights that they had. The parallel exists."[19] Representative Swift's sly allusions to Nazism were supplemented in late October by TV commercials that ascribed the most nefarious motives to term limits supporters:

"They want to end Social Security for our seniors . . ."

"They want to let oil tankers like the Exxon *Valdez* into Puget Sound . . ."

"They want to strip our state of our strength to protect ourselves . . ."

Coupled with a flurry of appearances by House Speaker Thomas Foley, the strategy worked. Proposition 553 lost 54 to 46 percent; but exit polls showed that 15 percent of those who voted against it would have supported term limits if other states had been similarly limited.

The supporters of the Washington LIMIT Campaign, though exhausted, were undaunted. They vowed to return in 1992 with a more strategic proposal to shift the question back where it belonged—reforming a corrupt Congress, without worrying about losing clout or water to California.

In truth, Prop 553 *was* flawed. Voters resented the retroactive nature of its limits, feeling that some of its sponsors were interested more in settling political scores against current incumbents than in instituting a major political reform. Its backers listened to the voters and came up with a new initiative for 1992. It lacked the retroactivity of Prop 553 and included a "trigger" clause that stipulated the limits would only take effect after ten other states had passed a similar law on their congressional delegation. Thus Washington State wouldn't risk losing its clout, and incumbent congressmen wouldn't be so terrified of imminent retirement.

The Term Limits Movement is back in business in Washington State and should be on the ballot in November 1992.

Nationwide, the campaign for term limits in 1992 is moving with a speed and degree of success that may force Congress to act on the issue in a few years. Three groups—Americans to Limit Congressional Terms, U.S. Term Limits, and Americans Back in Charge—are all actively helping state organizations to qualify initiatives for the ballot. Term limits should be on the ballot in November 1992 in California (for Congress), Wyoming, Washington State, South Dakota, North Dakota, Oregon, Ohio, Nevada, Nebraska, Michigan, Montana, Missouri, Florida, Arizona, and Arkansas. Together these fifteen states represent more than one-third of the nation's population. If you would like to contact one of the term limits groups in any of the above states, or other states where term limits activity is ongoing, please consult the appendix at the end of this book.

No one knows how many states will approve term limits in 1992, but if most of the initiatives on the ballot succeed, the political momentum for the idea may be irresistible. All candidates for Congress in 1992 have been asked to sign a pledge binding them to vote for term limits. When Grover Norquist of Americans for Tax Reform, convinced over one hundred members of Congress to take a similar pledge against higher taxes during the 1988 elections, he almost singlehandedly sank the 1990 budget agreement—only a few pledge takers were willing openly to violate their promise to the voters.

As with the tax pledge, several dozen incumbents have felt compelled to sign the term limits pledge even though many harbor doubts about being locked into a position. What made them sign was the fear of losing votes to a challenger who had signed. By forcing incumbents and challengers to take a stand on term limits, the political pressure will be ratcheted up with each passing election. Such pressure can often have unexpected results. Consider the Balanced Budged Amendment to the U.S. Constitution. Until early 1992, few thought it stood a realistic chance of passing Congress. Then, in a few short weeks, it was taken off the shelf and almost approved by two-thirds of both houses of Congress.

Term limits could be the next great constitutional change forced on our elected leaders by a groundswell of popular support.

# 12

# A BIPARTISAN REFORM

WHEN ALL OTHER ARGUMENTS against term limits fail, some politicians will be sure to trot out the charge that the movement is a front for conservatives and Republicans who want to use term limits to kick out liberals and seize control of Congress.

Well, if term limits are a creature of right-wing political pitchmen, they have attracted a lot of nonconservatives to their banner. The polls show that term limits are overwhelmingly popular with the American people. An October 1991 *Wall Street Journal*/NBC News poll found that Americans back term limits by 75 to 21 percent nationwide. Support cuts across income, party, ideology, race, and sex. Those earning less than $20,000 a year supported term limits by 77 to 16 percent. Democrats and blacks both gave term limits 71 percent support. Liberals favored them by 70 to 21 percent. Women backed them more than men.

Despite the broad-based nature of support for term limits, some still conjure up the right-wing bogeyman. Campaigning against a term limit proposal in his home state of Washington in 1991, Speaker Tom Foley charged that most of the support for it came from "extreme right-wing activists."[1] Ron Brown, chairman of the Democratic National Committee, agreed:

"term limits are a back-handed attempt by Republicans to get rid of Democrats they can't defeat at the polls."[2]

An anti-term limit treatise written by the Kamber Group, a Washington, D.C., consulting firm that often advises labor unions, put it even more bluntly:

"The term limitations movement is, at its leadership, organizational, and funding core, a desperate and calculated attempt by a cadre of frustrated Republican operatives, right-wing ideologues and conservative businessmen to wrestle away the Democrats' control of the U.S. Congress and as many state legislatures as possible. The proponents' long-term goal is to reverse the nation's political, economic and social directions. . . .Their refusal to be more forthcoming is understandable. Most citizens, after all, want better government, not a return to the pre-New Deal era for which many limiters long."[3]

Even though term limits are supported by all groups in society, it's true that their most visible advocates are conservative. That's partly because an organized campaign of intimidation and pressure mounted by Democratic leaders in Congress has prevented many prominent liberals from endorsing the idea. "The rank-and-file of the Democratic party favors term limits, as do I," former New York Mayor Ed Koch stated. "But I have to admit that if I were still in office, I might not have come out publicly in support of them because of pressure from party leaders who have a lot to lose if they become law."[4]

Given the pressure to squelch Democratic support for term limits, a surprising number of people in the party have endorsed them. They include Sens. Tom Daschle of South Dakota, Dennis DeConcini of Arizona, James Exon of Nebraska, and Harris Wofford of Pennsylvania; as well as Rep. Andy Jacobs of Indiana. Wofford used his support for term limits effectively in his campaign against Washington insider Richard Thornburgh. Paul Tsongas, who came in strong in the Democratic presidential primaries, now supports term limits.

"I used to oppose them, but it's an idea whose time has come," he remarked. "It has both pluses and minuses. It will, we hope, return us to the idea of citizen legislators who serve a few terms and return to private life. But we will also throw out the good with the bad. Still, I believe that before the decade is out it will become a reality in many states."[5] Gov. Bill Clinton is "personally opposed" to limits, but he has said he might support them in "five, six years" if campaign finance reform didn't make elections more competitive.[6] Even Gov. Mario Cuomo of New York is warming to term limits and says he is tempted to endorse them.

Sherry Bockwinkel, executive director of the Washington State term limit initiative, dismisses arguments that term limits only benefit conservatives. She notes that the authors of Washington's initiative, including herself, were largely liberal feminists and peace activists. The group that supplied much of their funding, Citizens for Congressional Reform, was indeed conservative but it had over nine thousand contributors in Washington State. "If our initiative was a right-wing plot, then you had to believe that the hundreds of bearded, countercultural volunteers we had were all incredible dupes," she concluded.[7]

One of the major reasons Bockwinkel and her friends wrote the initiative was to open politics up to many people presently frozen out of office by career incumbents. They include blacks, other minorities, and women. While women's national organizations don't endorse term limits, many of their feminist members in Washington State actively support them. Sherry Bockwinkel says, "I believe that women and people of color will have far more opportunity if incumbents have to move on. It will break up the old-boy network. All these other voices have been kept out, and when you take away the Incumbent Protection Machine, you will see more folks from diverse backgrounds running for office."[8] Fernando Guerra, a professor at Loyola Marymount University, agrees that term limits will mean greater opportunities for minorities. Nationwide, only 7 percent of those now elected to Congress are women or minorities. Almost all of them won their seats when they were vacant; they didn't dare challenge an entrenched incumbent.

"Incumbency is the glass ceiling of American politics," notes Kay Slaughter, the Democratic candidate for a special U.S. House election in Virginia last year.[9] Her GOP opponent opposed term limits. Former Rep. Shirley Chisholm, who in 1972 was the first black to run for a major party presidential nomination, is firmly committed: "I always said that I never intended to spend all my creative and productive years in the political arena. That's what is wrong with Washington now. Some of these guys have been there for years. You need an infusion of new blood and new ideas."[10] Colorado Rep. Ben Nighthorse Campbell, the only American Indian in Congress, backed a term limit measure in 1990 that restricted his own tenure.

Historically, term limits for Congress have been supported by some of the party's most prominent Democrats. Harry Truman believed term limits would "cure two maladies of democracy—legislative senility and seniority." John F. Kennedy endorsed the idea, noting with irony that those who opposed term limits for legislators were not at all eager to remove the two-term limit he faced as president.

Today, California Gov. Jerry Brown made term limits a key element in his populist presidential campaign against a "constipated" political system. "Term limits are a castor oil that democracy needs to take," he claimed. In 1990, while he was chairman of the California Democratic party, he refused to sign a party slate mailer against term limits. "My experience as party chair convinced me term limits are needed," he said. "I saw incumbents spend their time fund-raising and worrying about how to stay in office. It's time more candidates thought of politics as a calling instead of a career."[11]

Brown insists that arguments contending that legislative

staff and the unelected bureaucracy would become more powerful under term limits only prove that "we must curb the
excessive power of those political players as well." Both groups,
he notes, opposed term limits in his home state; the California
initiative included budget cuts that retired over seven hundred
legislative staffers.

Jerry Brown isn't the only populist Democrat with kind
words for term limits. Minnesota Sen. Paul Wellstone has
pledged to serve only two terms, but he thinks such limits
should be voluntary. If they are, they won't work. Sens. Dennis
DeConcini (D.-Ariz.) and Nancy Kassebaum (R.-Kansas) both
pledged to serve only two terms. Both are now in their third.

Another former Democratic governor who supports term
limits is Madeleine Kunin of Vermont, who retired in 1990
after three terms. "Political careerism has led people to con-
clude that politics is practically useless," she wrote. "I am
desperate to make politics come alive again. Breaking the
gridlock of incumbency could throw the doors open to new
people and new ideas that would make politics rewarding,
meaningful and fun. The shock could even rouse the
etherized American voter."[12] "The system needs a kick in the
rear," says former Colorado governor Richard Lamm, a leading Democrat. "Term limits have flaws, but they will provide
badly needed competition."[13]

John Lindsay, former mayor of New York and Democratic
candidate for president in 1972, says the high reelection rate
for House incumbents has convinced him that "you no longer
have effective competition." A term limit would at least provide "some way to sweep out the old wood."[14]

Democratic party apparatchiks are suitably worried about
such liberal defections and have tried to impose a party line on
term limits. The Democratic Congressional Campaign Committee quietly put out the word that it would blacklist political
consultants who advised candidates to back term limits and
told pollsters not to ask term limit questions. After they com-

plained about the blacklist, Alex Evans and Don McDonough, two Democratic campaign consultants from California, were assured by the DCCC that no such list would be kept.

While party intimidation has slowed support for term limits among many sitting Democratic officeholders, it has not gagged them all. In Massachusetts, the Democratic attorney general and secretary of state both favor term limits. Secretary of State Michael Connolly says that when he served in the legislature, "I was struck by the people who had been able to establish a niche of power, who literally and figuratively settled in with the idea they'd be there for a lifetime. That was a real detriment to good government." In Texas, Gov. Ann Richards says she "would be glad" to sign a bill limiting congressional and legislative terms.

Journalists find it easier than elected officials to express enthusiasm for term limits. Among them, several who will never be accused of being card-carrying Republicans, are *Washington Post* columnist Richard Cohen, syndicated columnist Richard Reeves, the *National Journal's* Neal Pearce, and *Time* magazine's Michael Kramer.

Hendrik Hertzberg, former speechwriter for Jimmy Carter and former editor of the *New Republic*, agrees term limits would mean the loss of some good legislators. However, he concludes that "it would be a cost worth paying to be rid of the much larger number of time-servers who have learned nothing from longevity in office except cynicism, complacency, and a sense of diminished possibility."[15] Columnist Ellen Goodman agrees: "We have to learn once again that ideal public service is, by definition temporary." Predictions, she notes, speak of as many as one hundred new members in the House after the 1992 elections. "If so, let them arrive with a new message. Go, hang around awhile, avoid the seductive charm of the cherry blossoms, do something. You can always go home again. You should go home again."[16]

Some longtime media opponents of term limits have

changed their minds in the wake of the House Bank scandal. The liberal *Seattle Times*, Washington State's largest newspaper, stunned its readers by endorsing term limits. In April 1991, WCVB-TV, the ABC affiliate in Boston whose liberal editorials have caused it to be called "the *Boston Globe* of the airwaves," denounced term limits as "the latest anti-government fad to sweep the country." But in October 1991 it switched sides and endorsed term limits for Congress: "We're not going to get [leadership] till we have a massive infusion of new blood."[17]

James Calaway of Texas is among those Democratic party activists who now favor term limits. Currently the national treasurer for the American Civil Liberties Union, Mr. Calaway was also chairman of the Democratic party's $15 million Victory Fund in 1988. He contends that term limits would mean "we're governed by citizens who go home after their service and not by permanent, elitist people who never leave office."[18] Other Texas Democrats who agree include Frances "Sissy" Farenthold, who cochaired George McGovern's 1972 national campaign, and Leonel Castillo, Jimmy Carter's director of the Immigration and Naturalization Service. Henry Cisneros, the first Hispanic mayor of San Antonio when he was elected in the early 1980s, also supports term limits.

Then there are the neoliberals, who, believing that centralized bureaucracies are the biggest obstacle to reforming government, are also warming to term limits. David Osborne, author of the best-selling book *Reinventing Government* speaks for many reform-minded liberals when he says, "Term limits are necessary to shake things up and disrupt the careerist mindset that leads to so much cowardice in public officials."[19]

While Speaker Tom Foley reacts to term limits as if his security blanket were being taken away, some House Democrats think it unlikely that term limits would mean large GOP gains in Congress. "People who say term limits are a Republican plot to oust incumbents and win their seats should know that a majority of open seats are won by Democrats," notes Rep. Andy Jacobs of Indiana, a lifelong Democrat.[20] Indeed, the Democratic party could actually be *helped* by term limits, according to former Oklahoma state legislator Cleta Mitchell, a self-described "liberal feminist" who heads the Term Limits Legal Institute in Washington. "Democrats must offer voters more than the simple powers of incumbency," she insists. "So long as our party is dominated by cynical veterans it will turn off the young people who are our party's future."[21]

Perhaps the most thoughtful liberal on term limits was a former member of Congress who is no longer with us. He was Ned Pattison, a Democrat who was elected from a Republican district in 1974 in the Democrats' landslide congressional victory. He was defeated in 1978.

Early in 1990, we contacted Mr. Pattison, one among several former Democratic representatives who had joined Americans to Limit Congressional Terms. Expecting a *pro forma* chat with him at his home near Troy, N.Y., we instead had several long talks with a man who had thought deeply about why government no longer was capable of doing the things he had wanted it to do while he was in Congress.

The seventy-five Democrats elected to the House in their party's 1974 landslide were part of a generation of idealistic post-New Deal liberals. They led a minirevolution in the House by ousting three powerful Southern committee chairmen and giving the Democratic Caucus the power to enforce party discipline. In large part, today's Congress is run by the forty-five or so members of the Class of '74 who haven't been defeated, retired, or gone on to other offices.

When he was first contacted by us in early 1990, Mr. Pattison was already ill with cancer. Perhaps his fatal illness prompted him to speak even more openly than he had in the past— Pattison was still a strong civil libertarian and social liberal. But unlike his colleagues who stayed in office, Pattison had grown suspicious of government's power and appalled at the "bloated beast" he felt Congress had become.

"There are simply a lot of things the government will never do well," he told us. "The problem neoliberals have today is that while they want to oppose special-interests, they are committed to voting more money for some of the most rigid, unresponsive bureaucracies ever created."

Ned Pattison was the first Democrat to represent his upstate New York district since the Civil War. Unlike many of his Class of '74 colleagues who trimmed their liberal sails, Mr. Pattison voted a strict liberal line in Congress. That record, coupled with an admission that he had smoked marijuana, cost him his seat in 1978. Mr. Pattison didn't follow the usual course by staying in Washington and lobbying his former colleagues. He served as a fellow at Harvard's Kennedy School of Government and then returned home to practice law.

Over time he abandoned liberalism and became interested in Jeffersonian ideas. He found the work of the libertarian Cato Institute "fascinating." He remained skeptical of conservatives because he believed they had their own ideological blind spots, namely blank-check spending on dubious military programs: "They couldn't see the Pentagon was like any other bureaucracy, the post office with guns."

A former county official, Mr. Pattison felt the federal government had grown beyond "human scale" and could accomplish few of its goals. The concept of federalism, he believed, had to be rescued from dusty history books. He admired Charles Murray's 1988 book, *In Pursuit of Happiness*, which argued that "little platoons" of communities and voluntary associations could best handle most social problems.

Mr. Pattison frequently returned to Washington as chairman of the Congressional Institute on the Future and to visit the now-graying Watergate babies. He found his friends finally wielding the levers of power, but enjoying it less and less. "I'd never thought I'd see the House gym so well used," he admitted sadly. "A lot of members realize they're engaged in play-acting, merely managing a bureaucratic empire they came to Washington to change."

Pattison didn't recognize the monster Congress had become. "I was present at the birth of the modern bureaucratic Congress, and I'm sure glad I'm not around now that it's grown up," he said. To him, that Congress had become a self-perpetuating institution. "They have voted themselves the perquisites and privileges they need to stay in office forever. They now mail nearly 1 billion pieces of mail a year, up from only 40 million in 1954. They get a staff of twenty-two in the House and up to eighty in the Senate. Their whole job is to make the boss look good and avoid taking real stands on issues."

The modern era of pork-barrel politics sickened Pattison. While "bringing back the bacon" for the district had been a time-honored American art form and relatively harmless, it had become much worse since federal grants-in-aid were developed in the 1960s. Now almost every bill, whether nominally about trade or appropriations, was "loaded up with unrelated provisions, giving money for beehive research in district X, extending a patent for some company in district Y, or paying for some intermodal highway demonstration project in district Z." And of course, all of this give-away was rewarded with campaign contributions. Pattison was convinced that the quid pro quo had become more pernicious than ever. He cited a Center for Responsive Politics survey which found that 20 percent of congressmen publicly admitted that fund-raising considerations compromised policy making.

Pattison came to believe that a fever was eating away at the health of Congress. It was rooted in the stupefying expansion of the bureaucratic state. Incentives for corruption were inevitable in any system where huge sums of money in endless categories were controlled and distributed by politicians and bureaucrats. In the year Ned Pattison died, a quarter of the nation's wealth—$1.2 trillion—was siphoned off to Washington. The result was a hot tub for middlemen, deal-makers, and arrangers.

Pattison was especially critical of the role he had played in building up Congress's power to micromanage the federal government. He recalled how he and his fellow Watergate babies perfected the skills of incumbency protection and constituency service. "There is no justification for constituency service the way it's done today," he told us. "Members don't act as ombudsmen waiting for people to come to them; they're out soliciting business. It's a bureaucracy within a bureaucracy. Over half of the staff works on constituent service to reelect the boss."

Congress's new definition of "constituent service" had broadened far beyond finding Aunt Millie's Social Security check; it now included Jim Wright-style arm twisting of regulators, all part of an unseemly trade for campaign contributions.

Congress clearly benefits from this system. First, members take credit for creating programs. Then they win votes and praise when they intervene on behalf of desperate constituents wrestling with the complex and unyielding bureaucracy that Congress has created. The contributions they receive in return keep the campaign merry-go-round running smoothly.

The Keating Five scandal didn't surprise Pattison. "Congress has become less of a deliberative body and more like a special-interest vending machine," he mourned. He believed that constituent services had replaced much of the legislating that members used to do. "Members love creating constituent service work for themselves—much of it illegitimate," he explained. "Constituent work lets them avoid the politically more risky role of legislators who must come up with real solutions."

As for solutions, Pattison thought that rules expanding "sunshine" laws might help. The sunshine laws currently in place allow "Congress to close the windows, pull the shades, and bar the door, lest the public see the light," according to Mark Leidl, a spokesman for U.S. Attorney for the District of Columbia Jay Stephens. Bob Dole has a bill that would make all contact between Congress and government officials a matter of public record. Dole thinks that if voters have a right to know who contributes to a member's campaign, they should also have the right to know on whose behalf their representatives makes telephone calls after the contribution is made.

Pattison had other ideas for congressional reform, such as the "sunset" law proposed by Sen. Edmund Muskie in the 1970s. This law would have automatically ended the life of a government agency unless specifically reauthorized.

But Pattison's favorite reform was term limits for Congress. "You wouldn't believe how many members privately tell me it's a good idea," he revealed. "They know the system is broken but they aren't willing to challenge it. If they knew they were in Congress for a limited time instead of as a career, it would act as a spur for some of them to try and change it." The best result of all concerned committee chairmanships. Normally divvied out on the basis of seniority, they would no longer largely go to jaded veterans with little real world experience but instead, perhaps, to members with actual experience in the subject area and a fresh outlook.

Other reforms that Ned Pattison favored included confining members to one district office, cutting current staff levels in half, and sharply limiting the amount of franked mail propaganda a member could send out. "Some 40 percent of all staffers now work back in district offices that are nothing more than disguised campaign headquarters," he reported.

Pattison's final reform proposal was to ban what he called "the dirty secret of American politics: gerrymandering." He wasn't sure what shape the reform should take, but he was intrigued by suggestions that formulas favoring compactness, a minimum disruption of county and city lines, and partisan competitive districts could be written into state constitutions.

Inspired to enter politics by John F. Kennedy, Mr. Pattison ended up having little use for his party's leaders. "I couldn't believe Dick Gephardt and his Japan-bashing," he said, shaking his head. "Even the White House isn't worth doing things like that." As for 1988 nominee Michael Dukakis: "Michael always confused governmental process with progress." George Bush, of course, fared little better in his estimation: "Bush is the consummate careerist who has only the courage of other people's convictions."

As he left the country restaurant where we had lunched, we asked if he was optimistic about Congress. "First, the voters have to realize that members only respond to what they think the people want. The people have to demand change. This term limit movement could go somewhere, people are that angry. I hope so. Even if it doesn't pass it will convince them that the game they're playing can't go on forever." Asked why he had been so candid about the mess in Washington, he answered, smiling, "It's said that a statesman is a politician who is no longer in office. Well, the definition of someone who tells it like it is could be someone who is soon checking out of life."

Three months later Ned Pattison was dead at the age of fifty-eight, the first of the Watergate babies to die of natural causes. He will be sorely missed.

# 13

---

# CONSULTING THE
# CONSTITUTION

---

SPEAKER OF THE HOUSE Tom Foley is normally a calm and
reserved person. But in 1991 he went ballistic when a term
limits initiative appeared on the ballot in his home state of
Washington. There was no way, he insisted, that an individual
state could impose term limits on its own congressional delegation. "The sponsors are totally wrong on this. I'm usually not
categorical on this but there is no, none, no legal case for the
other side. It constitutes a legal fraud on the public."[1]

Mr. Foley and other incumbents believe that if they repeat
this mantra—state term limits are unconstitutional—it will
somehow be true. They contend that 71 percent of the voters
of Colorado acted unconstitutionally when they limited their
federal legislators in 1990. And, ironically, they are backed up
by many of the same constitutional law experts who always
find new rights and new powers for the federal government in
the "penumbra" of the Constitution. But when it comes to
term limits their narrow reading of the founding document
would make a constitutional literalist blush. Lawrence Tribe, a
Harvard Law School professor frequently cited by congressional leaders, thinks "it is abundantly clear that qualifications for
federal office are matters of federal law as specified in the

171

Constitution . . . and it is quite doubtful that a state can add to the requirements for federal office."[2]

Terry Considine, the former state legislator who authored the Colorado limit, says simply that he will see his opponents in court. Knowing that Congress is unlikely to impose term limits on itself absent massive public pressure, he adds that many people falsely fear a "runaway" constitutional convention would have to be called if Congress refused to adopt an amendment. "Under our Constitution, the states are charged with regulating an effective political marketplace," he explains. "If each state imposes limits on its own federal officials, we can achieve our goal of a citizen Congress without a constitutional amendment."[3]

Considine notes that Article I, Section 4 of the Constitution gives the states the right to set the "time, places, and manner of holding elections for senators and representatives," although Congress may "at any time make or alter such regulations."

Opponents of term limits throw up a number of objections to Mr. Considine's "Colorado" plan. They argue that state limits violate the First and Fourteenth Amendment rights of voters, the Equal Protection Clause of the Fourteenth Amendment, and the Qualifications Clauses of the Constitution. The Supreme Court has held that the First and Fourteenth Amendments guarantee every citizen the freedom to vote, the right to have one's vote counted, and the right to associate with others to advance political beliefs. The Equal Protection Clause guarantees each citizen the equal protection of the laws. The Qualifications Clauses specify the age, citizenship, and residency requirements to serve in Congress.

As explained in chapter 11, the arguments against term limits based on the First and Fourteenth Amendments were disposed of by the California Supreme Court when it upheld that state's limits on state officeholders in 1991. California Assembly Speaker Willie Brown and others claimed that term limits discriminated against incumbents and thereby violated their right to equal protection of the laws under the Fourteenth Amendment. They also claimed that a "fundamental right to be a candidate for public office" could be found among the "associational rights" in the First Amendment. And they argued that voters in Willie Brown's San Francisco district were being denied their right to vote for him by an initiative most of them had voted against.

Knowing that half the nation's governors were covered by term limits and that the Twenty-second Amendment also limited the number of presidential terms, the state legislators tried to make a distinction between themselves and executive branch officials. They argued that "the patronage and military powers of an elected chief executive made long tenure in that position a threat to republican government."

California's highest court, however, rejected all of those arguments. In a 6 to 1 ruling upholding term limits, it said there was no inherent reason why governors and the president should have a limit imposed on them, while state legislators were allowed permanent tenure. Term limits don't restrict the right to vote for a candidate because of his party affiliation. And they don't prevent those sharing the same political creed from uniting and selecting a candidate to represent their interests. Therefore, they do not deprive voters of the freedom to associate with any particular party. Rather, they prevent citizens from voting for a particular candidate and only for a particular office. The restriction is furthermore imposed on all those who have served a certain number of terms— whether Republicans, Democrats, or Independents.

In rejecting all of the arguments against state term limits, the California court cited various U.S. Supreme Court decisions that give term limit supporters reason to believe state limits on federal representatives may also be constitutional. The Supreme Court has already held in a 1972 decision (*Bullock v. Carter*) that a particular candidate has no "fundamental right" to ballot access or to run for office. The Court and lower federal courts have upheld numerous state election laws restricting who can run for office. The right to vote does not guarantee that a citizen may vote for anyone he or she chooses, regardless of constitutional limits on qualifications or state laws regulating elections. Rather, it entitles the voter to have his or her vote counted in the election of those who are eligible to run.

Certainly federal candidates have frequently been kept off ballots. Larry Agran, former mayor of Irvine, California, ran for president in 1992 and met all of the constitutional qualifications to serve. But sixteen states declined to place his name on their presidential primary ballots for reasons having nothing to do with his constitutional qualifications. Some states simply declared he was not a "serious" candidate even though he participated in debates with Governor Clinton and Jerry Brown. Paul Tsongas did not appear on the ballot in Oklahoma because he failed to meet its election laws. He was also almost removed from New York's ballot for not fully complying with that state's Byzantine election code, which goes so far as to specify the type of paper clip that must bind petitions for ballot access. Tsongas ended up finishing second in the New York primary with 29 percent of the vote.

Nor do term limits conflict with the Equal Protection Clause of the Fourteenth Amendment In the past, the Supreme Court has overturned ballot access restrictions only if they discriminate against the poor or against new, small, or independent party candidates. The Court gives state legislatures the benefit of the constitutional doubt when they limit ballot access.

But even though the California Supreme Court demolished many of the legal arguments against term limits, it didn't address federal limits. That gives term limit opponents reason to hope that the courts will strike down state-imposed limits on the grounds they add another "qualification" for service in Congress.

Term limit opponents note that the courts have always ruled that neither Congress nor the states may add to or subtract from the age, residency, and citizenship requirements set forth in the Constitution. Term limits, they claim, add to the Qualifications Clauses, creating new minimum requirements that need to be met before a candidate may run for office. Therefore, they contend, a state cannot limit its own federal representatives.

But term limits aren't the same as qualifications that restrict access to office. Unlike the age, residency, and citizenship requirements, term limits don't prevent a nonincumbent from running for office. Nor do they prevent an incumbent who leaves office for a few years from running again. Nor, again, do term limits in any way modify the Qualifications Clauses of the Constitution.

States have broad powers, granted to them by the Tenth Amendment, to regulate the conduct of elections, short of violating the Constitution. The Tenth Amendment reads: "The powers not delegated to the United States by the Constitution, nor prohibited by it to the States, are reserved to the States respectively, or to the people." Congress has never acted to ban any term limits proposal.

William Mellor, head of the Institute for Justice in Washington, notes that the Supreme Court has recently renewed its interest in federalism. The Court clearly believes that various areas of the law are rightfully left to the states. Election law has traditionally been one of those areas.

The Court has long held that the electoral process must involve a lively competition of ideas, parties, and candidates, and be accompanied by a high degree of citizen participation. In 1974 in *Storer v. Brown*, the Supreme Court upheld a California law barring independent candidates in congressional races who had changed to independent status within eleven months of the election. The Court said that "there must be a substantial regulation of elections if they are to be fair and honest" and that the states' regulation under the Constitution of the "times, places and manner" of their congressional elections may include "the qualifications of candidates." Constitutional lawyer Stephen Glazier argued that in the current incumbent-protected political environment, where members of Congress are insulated from accountability, the Supreme Court's requirements for a robust competition of ideas, parties, and candidates does not exist. It is through that competition, the Court wrote in *Storer v. Brown*, that "the winner in the general election . . . [earns] sufficient support to govern effectively."

Later that same year, a Pennsylvania federal court used the *Storer* decision to uphold a state law blocking the independent candidacy of an incumbent Republican congressman who had lost in his party's primary. The court found that states can restrict access of congressional incumbents to the ballot by requiring a one-year waiting period before an incumbent who loses his party's primary can run again.

In a 1982 case, *Clements v. Fashing*, the federal courts upheld a Texas resign-to-run law that requires an official to quit a current office to run for another. The same reasoning was extended to uphold similar laws that prevented a New York judge and an Arizona county supervisor from running for Congress without first quitting their positions.

Term limits advocates argue that states have an inherent right to adjust their election laws to reflect local conditions. In most states, incumbents have an in-built advantage that skews the electoral process and makes elected officials less responsive to the will of the people—as, for example, Texas, where in 1990 an astounding twelve out of twenty-seven congressional incumbents faced no major party opposition. Term limits can eliminate this unfair advantage and make the electoral system more democratic. Viewed in this light, term limits do not alter the Qualifications Clauses of the Constitution. They merely ensure that real electoral competition, as envisioned by the Founding Fathers, actually takes place.[4]

The Supreme Court ruled in 1988 in *South Carolina v. Baker* that certain "extraordinary defects in the national political process might render congressional regulation of state activities invalid under the Tenth Amendment." The Court did not specify what it meant by the term "extraordinary defects" but the current near impossibility of defeating congressional incumbents in any year that doesn't have a House Bank scandal, and the fact that one out of five incumbents ran with no major party opposition in 1990 might qualify.

Given all this, Stephen Glazier believes that "the thrust of federal court decisions is that the actions of a democratically elected state government will not be frustrated by the 'no additional qualifications' clauses, if the state limits candidates for its congressional races in a way that doesn't offend freedom of speech or equal protection."[5]

Critics of Glazier's approach, such as Georgetown Law Center professor Walter Berns, cite the 1969 Supreme Court ruling in the case of *Powell v. McCormack* as proof that the courts would overturn state-imposed term limits. That case held that Congress could not refuse to seat Adam Clayton Powell, a member-elect who met the qualifications set forth in the Constitution. By not seating Powell, the Court found that Congress had added to the constitutional qualifications for office. "The *Powell v. McCormack* case clearly shows that term limits are a flagrant violation of the right of the people to choose whom they send to represent them," contends legal scholar Bruce Fein.[6]

But the point of the Court's ruling in *Powell v. McCormack* was that *Congress* was unable to exclude a member-elect who met the constitutional requirements. It was silent on the issue of state regulation. "*Powell* clearly limits what the House might do, but it does not necessarily answer the question of what a state might do," says A. E. Dick Howard, constitutional law professor at the University of Virginia.

Wallace Rudolph, constitutional law professor at the University of Puget Sound, says that the *Powell* decision set a minimum number of qualifications for holding a seat in Congress, but not a maximum. "Many states bar felons from running for office or even voting," he reports. "I don't see a state not allowing a felon on the ballot and the Supreme Court forcing it to put him on." Professor Howard agrees. He thinks the current Court will look favorably on a state's power to regulate access to the ballot if it does not explicitly go against the Constitution. "This Court certainly respects state power, courts, and institutions. If the issue is placed in terms of state interest, they might be inclined to uphold term limits."[7]

In addition, Terry Considine notes that Colorado's limit on federal officials do not take effect until the year 2002. No one will be prevented from running for reelection until then. "My sense," he says, "is that no one will have standing to challenge the term limit until 2002. Courts don't exist to hear hypothetical cases, and it's only when someone confronts a limit that they will have a sufficient stake in the outcome of a lawsuit to have standing to litigate it."[8] By that time, with any luck, the term limits bandwagon will be (or will have been!) irresistible.

Steven Ross, legal counsel to the House of Representatives, believes a lawsuit challenging the Colorado limit will soon be in the works: "I think an argument can be made that the injury begins for the members of Congress and their constituents right from the start, not twelve years later." David Miller, legal director for the American Civil Liberties Union of Colorado, is convinced a lawsuit would be accepted by the courts and plans to file one. One possible argument is that the Colorado decision unfairly limits the ability of incumbents to raise money, since contributors know they will be leaving office by a certain date.

Should the Supreme Court accept a challenge to the Colorado limit or that of some other state, how the Court will rule is unclear. Rep. Tom Campbell, former law clerk to Supreme Court Justice Byron White, thinks the near impossibility of defeating an incumbent today may convince the Court to allow voters to decide democratically that the only way they can feasibly remove incumbents is to limit their terms.

The notion that the courts will allow states to protect the competitive nature of the political process is, after all, an old one. Although Lawrence Tribe, Harvard Law school professor, opposes state-imposed term limits, he acknowledges that "few prospects are so antithetical to the notion of rule by the people as that of a temporary majority entrenching itself by cleverly manipulating the system through which the voters, in theory, can register their dissatisfaction by choosing new leadership." Tribe goes on to note that "courts have reviewed rather summarily laws that specify eligibility requirements for particular candidates . . . [A]fter all, there will ordinarily be some eligible candidates to represent any given political persuasion."9

Various states have acted on their own fundamentally to change their electoral systems. In 1988, for example, New Hampshire's legislature limited how much candidates for the U.S. House and Senate from that state could spend on their campaigns. No federal law on the issue exists, yet New Hampshire's law hasn't been thrown out by the courts.

Some states have imposed conditions on how their federal legislators are picked. The first was the practice of instruction, which was widespread in the United States until the 1850s and never subjected to constitutional challenge. In that practice, state legislatures required their U.S. senators to vote in accordance with the views of the majority of the state legislature; the legislatures believed that since the Constitution gave them the power to elect senators to Congress, they also had the power to instruct. New Jersey and Ohio, for example, instructed their senators to support Andrew Jackson's presidential program, and Vermont instructed its senators to "present anti-slavery resolutions to Congress." Some senators ignored instructions successfully. But others were forced to resign when they disobeyed their legislatures.[10]

The second precedent grew out of the battle for direct election of U.S. senators early in this century. The Constitution originally dictated that senators were to be elected by the state legislatures, not by the people. Leaders in the Progressive Movement of the late nineteenth century wanted to make Congress more immediately accountable by requiring that senators be chosen by the people directly, just as House members were.

The reformers bypassed the legislatures by using the new initiative process to get several states to pass laws for the popular election of their senators. These initiative laws set up direct party primaries for Senate candidates and often bound state legislators to vote for the winners of those primaries. By 1900, the direct election of senators had become part of the Democratic party's national platform.

The agitation for direct elections worked. By 1912 senatorial primaries took place in twenty-nine of the forty-eight states, and Congress finally bowed to the inevitable and ratified what was already the *de facto* practice in most of the country. It approved the Seventeenth Amendment to the Constitution—the direct election of senators—which was ratified the following year.

A similar grass roots effort using the initiative process could force Congress to pass another constitutional amendment to limit terms or, at the least, limit incumbency in some way. The popularity of term limits may force some members to vote in favor of them, despite their personal reservations. They might even be able to circumvent the limits themselves by establishing a "grandfather" clause exempting all current incumbents.

No one can predict with certainty the outcome of the term limits battle. But one thing is certain. The outraged citizens who want term limits will not sit idly by and wait for the courts to decide on state limits, nor will they take no for an answer. They will continue to search out ways to limit the power of incumbents regardless of how the constitutional arguments shake out.

Most of the term limits initiatives on state ballots in 1992 restrict the right of incumbents to run but do not impose a formal term limit that might run afoul of the Constitution. These initiatives tell an incumbent whose "term limit" is up that he must make way for someone else unless he chooses to run in the future as a "write-in" candidate. This would put incumbents at a disadvantage at the polls and ensure that incumbents and challengers compete on an even footing. If an incumbent were truly effective and popular, it would not be a crushing obstacle. True statesmen, that is, would be allowed to continue in office if they had genuine and overwhelming support. Two sitting U.S. House members (Ron Packard of California and Joe Skeen of New Mexico) won their *first* terms as write-in candidates. Surely incumbents running in a write-in campaign would have the resources to educate voters in the proper procedures for casting a write-in ballot.

A second term limitation option would require candidates to have "ballot statements" appear next to their names. Each candidate would have to answer the question: "Will you adhere to a _____ year term limit?" The answer would appear on the ballot along with the name of each candidate so that every voter would know where each stood on term limits. Candidates who promised to serve only a certain number of years and broke that pledge could expect retribution from the voters next time around.

Another restriction would allow incumbents to run after their term limit had expired but only if they first paid for distributing a reelection petition to all registered voters. It would require incumbents to obtain a certain percentage of voter signatures as a precondition to ballot placement. This restriction could also insist that incumbents use their petition to notify voters of their votes on key issues in Congress and to explain their votes. Many such ballot restrictions have been upheld by the courts.

Such alternate ways of limiting terms are likely to survive court challenges if a formal limit by the states is rejected. These optional forms of a term limit could, of course, be constitutionally overridden by the Congress, since the Constitution allows Congress to overturn state regulations. But legislators would have to alter what Americans have mandated by initiatives or through their legislatures and "would set themselves up for harsh—and perhaps politically fatal—criticism," says Trudy Pearce of Citizens for Congressional Reform.[11] "A majority of members of Congress would have to go on record as putting their own self-interest before a provision favored by two-thirds or more of their constituency," adds Stephen Glazier. Given its recent track record, it's doubtful Congress would take that risk.[12]

# 14

# AFTER TERM LIMITS:
# NONE OF THE ABOVE

EVERY YEAR each of the party caucuses in the House holds an annual retreat for its members at a resort location near Washington. In April 1991, the Republicans held theirs in Princeton, N.J., at an elegant conference center. During the meeting, we assembled an informal group of members for dinner as part of the job of reporting the event for the *Wall Street Journal.*

The goal was to discuss possible congressional reforms and gauge which the members were likely to support and which they considered dangerous and wrongheaded (in other words, a threat to their incumbency).

Over after-dinner drinks, the discussion began. As each reform was brought up, an informal vote was taken. There was general agreement in favor of minor campaign finance reform, changes in franking procedures, a ban on proxy voting in committees, and a bipartisan, professional House administrator. Then the reforms became tougher to sell. The members present were cool to the idea of banning gerrymandering of districts—turning the job over to a nonpartisan commission. With one exception, they opposed term limits. But what really got their dander up (one member's fists actually pounded the table) was the "None of the Above" ballot option. If

won the vote, a new election would have to be held with
new candidates. "Why, that means I could lose my seat to . . . to
an empty chair!" one member spluttered. Another remarked
that he "had never heard of a worse idea in my life."
Hmmmm. If that's how incumbents feel about the idea, it must
be good enough to consider.

NOTA, along with term limits, is another device on the
horizon that could open up elections to more political competition. Citizens fed up with the political status quo are already
preparing initiatives to add a None of the Above option to
ballots in Alaska and California.

The concept is simple. Let's say voters learn something
about both major candidates in the months after their nomination that disaffects them—makes them want to reject both of
them. If a plurality or majority of votes is cast for NOTA, a
special election would have to be held with new candidates.
The candidates who lost to NOTA would be disqualified from
the second race. Many states hold special elections quickly; in
such states, if NOTA were to win, say, a congressional race, it
shouldn't be difficult to hold a new election in time to seat a
new Congress in January. If people think allowing a vote for
NOTA casts the election in too negative a light, the ballot line
could instead read: "In Favor of a New Election."

Many voters would welcome this opportunity. In 1990, 52
percent of Texas voters told the Gallup Poll that, if possible,
they would likely vote for NOTA instead of either Republican
Clayton Williams or Democrat Ann Richards. Consider how
much Louisiana voters would have welcomed being able to
vote for None of the Above in their 1991 race for governor
between the racist David Duke and the rascally Edwin Edwards. In a Mason-Dixon Poll taken just before the vote, 66
percent of Louisiana voters wished the state had a None of the
Above line on its ballot. In a hypothetical runoff election
against Duke and Edwards, NOTA finished with 30 percent of
the vote.

Millions of Americans are tired of entering polling booths and having to choose the "lesser of two evils." Last year, in one out of five House districts they didn't even have that choice. Incumbents in those elections faced no major party competition.

It's time we learned a lesson from the former Communist nations of Eastern Europe on how to use NOTA to reinvigorate democracy. Both Poland and the Soviet Union have used a form of NOTA. In the 1989 semifree elections in Poland, voters were able to cross off the names of candidates they rejected—every name if they wished. This allowed them to defeat even the unopposed Communist incumbents, such as the sitting Polish prime minister, because they didn't get the required absolute majority, or because less than half the electorate voted. In the Soviet Union, new elections with new candidates had to be held in two hundred out of 1,500 races for the Congress of People's Deputies. In the runoff elections, over one hundred Communist incumbents were defeated. Boris Yeltsin has said the Soviet's version of NOTA "helped convince the people they had real power even in a rigged election and played a role in building true democracy."[1]

The U.S. has some experience with NOTA. In the 1992 presidential primaries, 31 percent of voters in South Dakota chose to vote for "Uncommitted Delegates" rather than President Bush. In the Democratic primaries, the uncommitted delegate slate routinely won 15 percent or more of the vote. In Kansas, an actual None of the Above line was on the ballot and it drew 16 percent, finishing ahead of Jerry Brown. The newly formed California Green party allows its primary voters a "None of the Above" choice in selecting party nominees. In June 1992, in a Los Angeles state assembly district, the NOTA line beat the one candidate on the ballot, 55 to 45 percent.

Many states also use a version of NOTA for judicial elections: sitting judges must win confirmation from voters in an up-or-down referendum. The vast majority of judges win confirmation, but they can lose if voters believe they are making the laws rather than merely applying them, as witness California's former Chief Justice Rose Bird.

Nevada put a nonbinding None of the Above option on its ballots in 1976. That year, it won a GOP congressional primary. In 1980, NOTA narrowly lost to Jimmy Carter in the Democratic presidential primary, but beat out Ted Kennedy for second place. In 1990, it came in second in both primaries for governor. But since Nevada's law does not require a new election if NOTA places first, NOTA is strictly a symbolic protest vote. That explains why present support for NOTA in Nevada is usually in the single digits. Even so, NOTA has had an impact on Nevada politics. Don Mello, a former state legislator who authored the law providing the ballot option, says that if NOTA wins the candidate who finishes second is humiliated. Mello says a significant NOTA vote "forces the winner to undergo a reality check, and if he was falling down on the job he usually walks the straight and narrow after that."[2]

Political scientists are intrigued by the idea of offering voters the option of NOTA. Curtis Gans, head of the Committee for the Study of the American Electorate, favors the idea. So does Seymour Martin Lipset, noted political scholar at Stanford's Hoover Institution. Lipset says NOTA would be an American version of the "no confidence" vote that frequently brings down parliamentary governments in Europe.

Giving voters the power to veto candidates would help combat the growing anticompetitive arsenal of incumbents, which offends many on both the Right and the Left. NOTA has been endorsed by the *Nation* magazine and the *Boston Globe* on the Left. On the Right its supporters include the *Wall Street Journal* and the *Manchester Union-Leader* in New Hampshire. Nackey Loeb, editor of the *Union-Leader*, jokes that NOTA "is the only issue we've ever agreed on with the *Boston Globe* and Ralph Nader."[3] John McClaughry, a Republican state senator in Vermont, has introduced a bill that would create a NOTA line on the state's ballot. Ralph Nader believes a NOTA with teeth could also increase voter turnout by giving disenchanted citizens a chance to vote "against" the existing candidates and "for" a new election.[4]

Tony Schwartz, a political consultant in New York, is so taken with the NOTA idea that he has come up with a sample political commercial that could be run by citizens dissatisfied with the candidates who are running:

> Many Americans don't have health care, jobs, or adequate public schools.
> Taxes go up while businesses shut down. Who's going to fix this mess?
> Republicans, Democrats, the White House? Let's choose.
> Who was not tainted by the Savings and Loan scandal? Clearly, NOTA.
> Which candidates refuse to be swayed by PAC money? Clearly, it's NOTA.
> Which elected officials do not raise taxes, do not put image above issues or make promises that are impossible to keep?
> The choice then is clear.
> At the voting booth select NOTA. NOTA. A reliable option. Because if the candidates won't change, we've got to change the candidates.
> Paid for by the None of the Above Committee.

NOTA would be far more effective than campaign-finance reform in reducing the overwhelming advantages of incumbency. In many races, second-rate incumbents win by beating third-rate challengers. With NOTA, a sitting officeholder could lose an election and give another candidate a chance even in a hopelessly gerrymandered, one-party district. And if

NOTA just came close to winning, even the most entrenched incumbents might be forced to rethink their positions and inject some needed humility into their thinking.

Adding NOTA to the ballot may also improve the nation's abysmal voter turnout. NOTA might even discourage highly negative campaigning, since candidates would be running *for* the approval of voters, and not just to offend fewer people than their opponents. When confronted with the option of bad v. worse, NOTA would allow people to say, "Give me a better choice." Isn't that one of the things that American democracy should be all about?

# 15

# THE ROAD FROM HERE

JANUARY 3, 2001. The millennium had come.

Timothy J. Burger, editor of the *Washington Post*'s daily "Capitol Chronicles" and Pulitzer prize-winning congressional correspondent, looks with amazement at the electronic tally board over the west entrance to the House chamber. Kimi Gray, a large, confident-looking black woman, is on her feet a few feet away in the aisle leading to the "well" of the House of Representatives. She calmly surveys the pandemonium and then glances up at the press gallery above the Speaker's rostrum. Burger catches her eye and she responds with a smile and a wink.

The vote was 217 to 217 as Mrs. Gray carefully inserted her small plastic voting card into the voting device on the back of the chair alongside the aisle and pressed the button marked YES. A roar erupted from the galleries and Cong. Colin Powell, retired chairman of the Joint Chiefs and newly elected representative from the state of New York, rose from his seat alongside the center aisle and acknowledged the cheers of his allies.

Mrs. Gray was an unlikely figure to play such an historic role during the first few days of the new millennium. Along with Representative Powell and over two hundred other freshmen members of the 107th Congress, this vote to select the new

189

Speaker was her first in this hallowed hall. It was certainly one of the most difficult she would ever cast, but she was sure she had done the right thing.

She was typical of the new faces in the battle for political reform in the nineties—an apostle of black empowerment, preaching to anyone who would listen that the promises of the Great Society had destroyed the economic basis of urban America, replacing the vigorous economic core of our cities with a socialized structure as flawed as in any Soviet state.

It was, ironically enough, the collapse of those former Soviet republics and their rediscovery of freedom, self-government, and private property that had opened the eyes of so many Americans to the plight of our cities. Kimi compared the decline of communism with the abject failure of decades of government housing programs, urban development "action grants," and "model cities" boondoggles, that had only empowered bureaucrats and their "experts," while they destroyed the social and fiscal fabric of our cities.

Kimi's route to Congress was as unconventional as her background. Past citizen of the projects, she was now part of the nation's first Citizen Legislature in over a century. Like so many of her colleagues milling about on the floor of Congress, she was anything but a professional politician. She was, in fact, proud to call herself an amateur in Congress, but a professional in life.

The politicians had seen this day coming for over a decade. They had known that the term limits train was coming—ever since 1990, when state initiatives had succeeded in California, Oklahoma, and Colorado. Then, in 1992, more than a dozen key states had scheduled term limits referenda, and the movement became a true revolution as the fall elections approached. November 3, 1992—Election Day. Who can forget the rollercoaster ride that evening as the political forces of the past and the future clashed, signalling the start of an historic struggle to control Congress and our nation's destiny.

All year long the pundits had predicted that the elections of 1992 would "throw the bums out." Months earlier, scores of legislators had announced their early retirement, though few confessed that they were leaving to cash out their campaign treasuries while they still could. Political experts predicted that the voters' wrath would be felt at the polls. Several veteran members had already lost primaries, and everyone was getting ready for an electoral earthquake.

But election night began disappointingly. As soon as the polls closed in New York, the networks reported that, on the basis of exit polls, most House incumbents, including notorious check-bouncers Stephen Solarz (743) and Edolphus Towns (408), had been reelected. Even Sam Donaldson, ABC's liberal correspondent, professed surprise. "Looks like some of these 'bums' in Congress still know how to win elections," he proclaimed.

Within an hour, word came from Georgia that Newt Gingrich (24 bad checks) and John Lewis (125) were victorious, and that Pennsylvanians had reelected Bill Goodling (430) to his tenth term.

By ten o'clock, McEwen (166), Stokes (551), and Oakar (213) were celebrating in Ohio, Ford (388) in Tennessee, Kika de la Garza (284) in Texas, Conyers (273) in Michigan, Clay (328) in Missouri, and even self-righteous Joe Early (140) in Massachusetts. The public could see the dimensions of the disaster. The incumbents were winning once again.

But the mood in living rooms across the country changed as the results of term limits initiatives started to come in. This was a different voice, a different message, coming from voting booths across the country. A cry for real change—and the first shout came from Florida.

It was almost nine o'clock when CNN declared that term limits had won and went live to Orlando for the victory celebration of "Eight is Enough," the feisty campaign that had fought to amend Florida's constitution and hold their politicians to eight consecutive years in office. Two-thirds of Florida's voters had cast their ballot for term limits. It was a rout and the night was still young!

Phil Handy, chairman of "Eight is Enough," gave the first of many term limits "victory speeches" that America would hear that evening:

"America has had enough! Enough arrogance, enough corruption, enough propaganda, enough pomposity, enough waste, enough deception, enough spending, enough taxes, and enough 'politics as usual' in Tallahassee and Washington. We're tired of congressmen-for-life who bribe us with our own money to keep themselves in power. Enough is enough—and Florida's voters have spoken: 'Eight is Enough!' "

From ABC's hectic "Election '92—Campaign Central," David Brinkley calmly remarked, "I think we're watching tonight the beginning of a true political revolution. Yeltsin and Gorbachev probably have more understanding of what's happening here than Clinton and Bush."

George Will couldn't help commenting on the obvious historical paradox. "All those victorious incumbents tonight must feel like the hapless William Sheldrick Conover II, who once had a similar election night. He was a congressional candidate in a special election on April 25, 1972, to fill a vacant seat, but he also had to run that same day in a primary to pick contestants for the general election later that year. It was the classic 'good news, bad news' outcome: He won the special, but lost the primary, and his career as a congressman was over just as it was getting started."

The victorious incumbents had won the same way they always had—by outspending their challengers. Some, like Bill Green, David Bonior, or Solarz, spent over a million dollars to get reelected. Others, like Dan Rostenkowski, John Dingell, Henry Waxman, and Gingrich, relied on the clout of their committee or party assignments. The rest just bragged about all the pork they carried with them when they waddled back home or the "friends" they'd made after years of selfless constituent "service."

The term limiters had little money, less clout, and no pork at all. Their national political campaign was the only one with a negative quid pro quo. "Contribute to us," they might have said, "and every politician will throw you out of his office." And yet, they were winning.

Within hours, CNN's big "Congressional Term Limits" map started to fill with color. Blue states appeared if a term limit referendum passed. Red was the sign of defeat. As America went to bed that evening, there were no red states.

In the House and Senate 359 incumbents were up for reelection that evening and only twenty-eight went to bed knowing they had lost. But they were restless about California's referendum on congressional term limits. They knew it would be a nightmare.

It was after midnight in the East before the California outcome was clear. CBS was the first to report the result. Correspondent Maria Shriver was at the victory party in Los Angeles. "Californians have just told the members of the House of Representatives that this was their last century in office," she declared. "The Congressional Term Limits Referendum is passing with nearly 60 percent approval and it means that, from now on, no one from California can serve more than six years in the House of Representatives nor more than twelve years in the Senate."

Behind her at the podium was the familiar face and physique of Arnold Schwarzenegger, mascot of the California campaign. The "Terminator" had a question for Congress: "Do you guys get the message? Hasta la vista, baby!"

The slogan for the term limit movement all year had been "Congress—They just don't get it," and every turn and twist of the stories from Washington confirmed it. Members seemed to be following some diabolical script proving how inane and corrupt they had become. Each newly uncovered scandal elicited a knee-jerk cover-up response, followed by stonewalling, defiance, and appeals to the courts for protection and delay. They were blind to their own reality, lost on a political treadmill pushing them toward oblivion, destined to fan the flames of envy, resentment, and ridicule that were destroying their palace of privilege.

Ten states passed term limits referenda that evening. One, Arizona, by a margin of 3 to 1. Now the term limits train was rolling at full speed and Congress would never be the same again.

Senate and House leaders promptly argued that these limits were unfair, undemocratic, and unconstitutional. But winning arguments wasn't the issue—keeping power was.

The leaders of the 103rd Congress pretended that nothing had changed. But in January, over a hundred new congressmen (and more than a dozen new senators) took the oath of office, the largest freshmen class since 1949—and most of them had promised to support term limits

The new reality in Congress was that nearly a third of all members represented states that had passed term limits initiatives. If added to the freshmen, it meant that more than half the House members were "theoretical" supporters who would, in all probability, sign a discharge petition and force the issue to a vote on the floor.

More than twenty-five different versions of a constitutional amendment were formally proposed in the first three weeks of the new Congress. Thus, when the president delivered his State of the Union Address in late January, he knew that most of those in the room would welcome or, at least, understand the wisdom of his words.

"I stand before you tonight," he said, "limited to eight years in office by the Constitution's Twenty-second Amendment. It is time for you to apply the same principle to yourselves. We need an amendment limiting congressional terms. Listen to your constituents—Democrats, Republicans, and Independents—they all agree. They want Congress again to become a Citizen Legislature."

Before long, a Congressional Term Limits Caucus was formed. They chose the ornate Mike Mansfield Room in the Capitol to establish their beachhead. There, they held their first press conference and presented their bold agenda.

Debating and voting on a term limits amendment was to be the first order of business, they declared. They urged the Judiciary Committee to hold hearings immediately and, in case they refused, announced that a "discharge petition"(a rarely used parliamentary technique to allow a majority of the House to overrule the leadership) was being formally intro-duced to gather the 218 necessary signatures to bring the question to the floor.

Caucus Chair Scott Klug, first elected in 1990 on a term limits platform, concluded the press conference by turning his back to the television cameras and pointing to the framed engraving of President Washington's Farewell Address that hung on the north wall of the room.

"George Washington set the standard for public service in America two centuries years ago. With the eloquent words engraved on this historic document, he limited his own term in office. Can't we be as patriotic today, as humble, as willing to yield our power, return it to people from whence it comes? Isn't it time for us to do the right thing?"

For months, the nation had fumed as Congress stalled. How could they be so arrogant, the people wondered. Now, public attention focused on the discharge petition.

Under House rules, since the petition was a "secret" docu-ment it was difficult to confirm how many had signed—it slowed down the whole process—but eventually, the word got out that the magic total—218—was close. Hill veterans were confident, however, that the term limits movement could be derailed by their own last minute parliamentary maneuvers.

Faced with an imminent discharge resolution, the Judiciary Committee decided it was time for a preemptive strike. Its members would hold hearings on their version of term limits, and in the process win more time.

On into 1994 dragged the term limits fight. The Judiciary Committee's proposal was for an eighteen year term limit, but with a provision that allowed further years of "service" after two years absence. The prospect of a long career interrupted by a short sabbatical, perhaps as ambassador to the Bahamas, was the new ideal. Even Jamie Whitten, after more than five decades in the House, could live with these limits.

Proponents from the dozen or so states that had already passed initiatives were outraged. Eighteen years was ridiculous, especially with the "out-and-back-in" loophole.

"That's like telling an alcoholic he can only have fifty drinks a day," said Sherry Bockwinkel, leader of the Washington State term limits campaign.

The public mood was clearly for a limit with teeth. Sixty percent of the country favored a limit of six years or less—and a quarter of those wanted a limit of only one term in both the House and the Senate!

And almost everyone, outside of Congress, wanted the limit to be a lifetime ban, rather than just a limit on years of consecutive service. "Otherwise, they won't really be limited, they'll just have to take a two-year vacation, probably at our expense, every decade or so," testified Frank Eizenzimmer, from Oregon's L.I.M.I.T.S (Let Incumbents Mosey Into The Sunset).

But the deck was stacked against the Term Limits Caucus. The "No-Limit Limit," as the official resolution came to be called, passed by 5 to 2, with Pat Schroeder abstaining. Rep.

Bill McCollum's amendment to shorten the limit to twelve years also only got two votes.

The full Judiciary Committee quickly ratified Rep. Don Edward's masterful work in the subcommittee, even in the face of rising public anger and cynicism. A *Wall Street Journal* editorial complained:

"The Judiciary Committee's No-Limit Limit is a fitting monument to a Congress that has given us No-Budget Budgets, No-Program Programs, No-Tax Cut Tax Cuts, and No-Reform Reforms. Last year, by our count, 98 percent of all the bills introduced in the House were No-Bill Bills. During the campaign last fall, all we got in most districts were No-Contest Contests. Reminds us, too, of those Non-Bank Banks and the No-Crop Crop subsidies. It's time to tell the No-Justice Judiciary Committee and our No-Policies Politicians that we know better. No-thanks."

Fortunately, the Term Limits Caucus was prepared. Throughout the hearings, they had circulated another "discharge petition" to win an "open rule" on the scheduled deliberation of the Term Limits Amendment when it reached the floor. On April 28th they got the 218th signature, compelling the Rules Committee to permit unbridled debate and amendments on the House floor.

The stage was set for confrontation. It was now a question of will. One side wanted to protect their careers—their most valuable possession. The other side sought to save Congress from itself and free the government from gridlock. In a sense, it was a fight between Congress, the institution and what it stood for, and its members, their careers, their privileges, and their concept of self-worth. At this point, no one knew which would win—the institution or the individuals.

For ten straight days the debate raged and the old bulls of Congress brought forth all the worn out arguments against term limits.

But the public had heard it all before. Ten days of televised debate on term limits convinced them even more about the need for limits. These guys were their own worst enemies.

Then, a new NBC/*Wall St. Journal* poll was released: 84 percent of those polled wanted term limits. How could Congress refuse?

Finally, the battle was drawn. The Term Limits Caucus had agreed to unite behind a single, tougher alternative, known as the Jacobs-McCollum substitute. It was simply worded, without any ambiguity or disingenuousness. It said:

> Resolved, by the people of the United States of America. No person who has been elected to the Senate two times shall be eligible for election or appointment to the Senate. No person who has been elected to the House of Representatives three times shall be eligible for election to the House of Representatives.

For nearly three hours early that afternoon, Democrat Jacobs and Republican McCollum managed the floor debate leading up to a critical, procedural vote to replace the no-limit limit with their tougher substitute. As the clock approached the agreed-upon time for the actual vote, Representative Jacobs went into the well to offer his final thoughts.

"I know this is a difficult vote for many of you—it is for me because it's never very satisfying opposing my party's leaders," he began. "Many of you may be thinking of your families and the security and comforts you want for them, or the work you've put into your careers and the pride you feel each time you see your name light up on the voting roster high on the wall behind me.

"But let me shift your thoughts instead to the 550,000 citizens who look at you as something more. They, too, have families, careers, and pride of place. But they also have you. You work for them. You are their representatives.

"We all know how they feel and what they want you to do here today. They don't want business as usual. They don't want a no-limit limit. They want real change. They want real reform.

"Think about how you would feel if you were one of them—ordinary citizens untouched by fame, power, and privilege. If someone else were your representative in this Congress of confusion and crisis, how would you want him or her to vote this afternoon?

"You know what to do. You know it's time to do the right thing."

There was a awkward second or two of introspective silence—then cheers and shouts of approval. After a few minutes of thundering applause the chamber again became hushed. Everyone awaited the one voice still to be heard, that of the Speaker. Tradition provided him with the privilege of having the last word. His was a bitter speech in defense of the status quo.

"Life is full of limits," he opened, "limits on how fast, how long, how far, how rich, how much fun, and how much work something or someone should be. Today, we decide how we limit our power, and what limits we place on the power of experience in Congress.

"We all know that people are frustrated with Congress and angry that it doesn't work better. But passing this draconian substitute resolution won't solve those problems; it'll just pass them on to a bunch of newcomers—people who may be less experienced, less dedicated, and less familiar with the traditions of Congress.

"Don't you understand all that this institution represents? Don't you remember its moments of greatness, its eloquence, its heroism? Don't you care if this is changed? If we allow this intemperate proposal to pass, we turn our backs on decades of growth and professional development. We return to the days of spittoons and country hicks. We abandon our ideals and embrace the most inexperienced among us. We surrender to a modern mob of reformers. As a result, this country will lose its greatest institution—its Congress.

"I know you will stand up to this challenge. I know you will vote down the substitute resolution."

Many of the members rose to their feet to give the Speaker a long and respectful round of applause. Only a few revealed the emotion that almost all of them felt. The agony of the vote was now at hand.

The Speaker intoned: "The vote is on the amendment in the form of a substitute to H.J.R. 101. All those in favor of the substitute, vote Aye, those opposed, Nay."

The bells across the south side of Capitol Hill were sounded, but few members had to be summoned to the chamber. They were there, prepared mentally, psychologically, and politically as best possible for the most important vote of their lives. As a measure of the historic nature of the moment, more than thirty senators watched quietly from the sidelines. They knew their careers were also at stake.

The members bunched around the voting machines throughout the chamber, anxious to cast their votes and take their seats. This ordeal was not something you wanted to endure standing up.

Quickly, the pattern appeared. Within sixty seconds, the tally board showed 112 in favor, 108 against. After five minutes more, the vote was 209 to 202. Then, the advancing numbers began to slow. 210. 215. 216. 217. The room held its breath. The board flashed 218! The substitute had succeeded. The No-Limit Limit was dead. After the fifteen minutes normally allotted for voting by electronic device the tally stood at 221-214.

The Speaker looked anxiously at Judiciary Chairman Jack Brooks who circled his finger over his head to urge him to keep the vote open for a minute or two more, as he tried to find someone who would change his or her vote. But only one succumbed to his desperate entreaties and, finally, the Speaker had to drop the gavel, conceding the final result: 220 to 215.

Quickly, the Speaker moved to the next step in the elaborate parliamentary process: final passage of the amendment, as revised by the Jacobs-McCollum substitute. He wanted to strike quickly, before the Term Limits Caucus could regroup.

"The question is on agreeing to the resolution, H.J.R. 101. All those in favor, please signify by saying Aye."

A roar of "Ayes" ricocheted around the chamber.

"Those opposed, signify by saying Nay."

Another roar, but clearly not so loud.

"In the opinion of the chair, the Nays have it. The resolution is defeated," the Speaker optimistically declared.

"Mr. Speaker, Mr. Speaker," screamed Jacobs and McCollum from different microphones, as a chorus of "Vote" echoed across the room.

"For what purpose does the gentleman from Indiana rise?" the Speaker asked.

"On that, I request a recorded vote," declared Jacobs.

"So ordered," conceded the Speaker. "The vote will be by electronic device."

Again the bells rang and members rushed to feed their little "credit cards" into the voting machines. This time they all knew the stakes. This was the big enchilada.

No psychologist can pretend to understand the voting behavior of 435 independent egos as big as the ones in that room.

You'll hear talk of a politician's hierarchy of needs and how, in special cases, he will sacrifice perceived self-interest to some other, higher cause. Perhaps it's a greater national goal, some imbedded moral or religious value, or a special personal objective, like the chance to leave his footprints where no one has ever been before.

Some argue that these moments also reflect their own unique destiny. Maybe they are all here as players in some grand and noble human drama, guided by a divine director who steers with an invisible hand. Predestined or not, Congress that day delivered itself from what it had become.

The House passed the Term Limits Amendment, 302 to 143. A few days later, the Senate followed suit, 79 to 21.

Ratification came quickly. State legislatures discovered a self-interest in limiting congressional terms, so by November 1995, twenty-seven states had already ratified the amendment. Early the next spring, ten more states gave their affirmation and, finally, Pennsylvania became the thirty-eighth to ratify the proposed amendment. Thus, on April 15, 1996, the Twenty- seventh Amendment became part of the U.S. Constitution. Taxation, that year, came *with* representation.

But the effects of the new amendment began even before it was ratified. Congress quickly began a flurry of institutional reforms—and more.

Among other reforms: the anachronism of the nonvoting delegate from the District of Columbia was abolished when Congress approved the District's marriage with Maryland; the frank for anything other than reply correspondence to current constituents was killed; and congressional pensions for anyone elected after 1994 were eliminated.

The 104th Congress also passed the landmark Entitlement Reform Act, making every dollar of spending, from Social Security to Veterans' Disability payments, subject to recorded votes each year. This was followed by the Infrastructure Investment and Funding Act of 1996, which helped build the automated highways, airports, and municipal infrastructure that, with the help of competitive private sector management and variable fee-for-service payment systems, contributed so much to America's urban renaissance.

The prospect of hundreds of competitive congressional elections every other year also roused American citizens from their decades of political dormancy. In 1997, two new political parties were successfully launched. One, the so-called Contractual party, fathered the theories of accountable political management—holding politicians legally, not just politically, responsible for the promises they make.

The other, the Network USA party, founded by computer genius Bill Gates, revolutionized the way government "interfaced" with the consumers of its services. Their recent Electronic Convention had more than 14 million Americans on-line with their personal computers and concluded with the selection of 535 congressional candidates as well as more than thirteen thousand nominees for state and local offices. Their "PC-Citizen" series of government-user software led everyone to question the most fundamental traditions of our archaic centralized bureaucracies.

By 1998, less than half of all Americans identified themselves as Democrats or Republicans. Both parties were associated with the career politicians of the seventies and eighties. Anyone with more than three or four years on a legislative payroll in Washington or a state capital, whether as an elected official or staff member, was considered too out-of- touch to be electable. Of those elected to Congress that fall, 60 percent had at least twenty years of private sector experience, and for the first time in over fifty years, less than a third of Congress had graduated from law school.

There were still defenders of the old "Congress without limits." One, James Glassman, former editor of *Roll Call* and lifelong defender of opulent congressional lifestyles, even ran for Congress from Maryland's 8th District. The thousands of retired staffers and former members living in the affluent suburbs of Washington helped him win the open seat in 2000.

Had term limits not been enacted, of course, he would have faced an entrenched incumbent and would never have been elected.


So now, on this cold January afternoon early in the bright new century, Congress has chosen its new Speaker, a citizen-soldier-congressman and one of the founders of the Contractual party. Kimi Gray looks up at Colin Powell as he ascends to the Speaker's chair, once more proud of her country and optimistic about its future.

Speaker Powell stands erect as the room fills with the applause of his allies and former opponents. He is a man they all respect. Finally, he speaks:

"Thank you, thank you. You know how proud and honored I am to have been chosen by you, the representatives of nearly 300 million Americans.

"Today we face our collective duty to govern this nation for the next two years. Each of us, I know, has dedicated himself to twenty-four months of selfless service to his nation. For all of us, it will be the journey of our lives, a time when we dig deep into our souls and find our wisest thoughts, our warmest compassion, and our most cherished principles.

"We will also need our common sense in order to understand our limits. Our political power is limited. Our time in office is limited. Our treasury, our arsenal, and our lives are limited.

"But there are no limits on our people and what they can accomplish in this new century. We cannot let them be limited by government's limits, or dependent on its priorities or philosophies. Our task is to represent them within the limits they have set and try, as best we can, to do the right thing.

"I have but one modest proposal as we begin this 107th Congress. Let us all forget about reelection. We have enough to do without fund-raising, press conferences, and campaigning day in and day out. Let's just do our job. Debate, argue, analyze, investigate, theorize, propose, and deliberate. And then, enact the laws, appropriate the funds, and oversee our government. That's our job. Let's do it.

"If we do it well, we'll earn something more important than any reelection and something Congress lost sight of for a long time. We'll earn the respect of our fellow citizens. Let's wait until we're done before anyone calls us 'the Honorable.' Maybe, then, we'll have earned it."

The next day, he met with President-elect Cheney at Blair House. They had been good friends for over a decade and he wanted to extend a welcoming hand in friendship, even though it was clear they had many differences.

"Your administration and the new Congress have a special opportunity these next few months," Powell began. "It's almost as though we were going on a honeymoon—and I had a present for you. You have my word that Congress will consider any proposal you submit without prejudice, permit full debate, and allow an up-or-down vote on any element of your legislative agenda.

"It's been a long time since Congress and the White House worked as allies. I think we both have some bitter memories of the nitpicking, second-guessing, and micromanaging we endured over the years. We've got an historic chance to change that for good. Why don't we give it a try?

"I've already announced that I'm only here for one term and have no further political ambition. So don't worry about short-term politics. Let's both just work together for our country."

The president-elect got up, walked to the window, looked across Pennsylvania Avenue at the White House, and then responded softly:

"Colin, I've already decided to announce in my Inaugural Address that I'm only going to stay in that beautiful house over there for four years. I don't want to worry every day about which way the wind is blowing either. Lord knows, we have enough to do without forever fretting about getting reelected.

"You're right. We can make a difference. This is going to be the American century. May God bless us both."

Colin turned to leave, extended his hand and said, "I'm sure He will, Madame President. He already has."

President Lynne Cheney could only smile.

# ENDNOTES

## Preface

1. Robert Cwiklik, *House Rules* (New York: Villard Books, 1992).

## Chapter 1

1. "Congressional Micromanagement: Domestic Policy," in Gordon S. Jones and John A. Marini, eds., *The Imperial Congress* (New York: Pharos Books, 1988), p. 133.
2. Interview, April 18, 1990.
3. Hendrik Hertzberg, "Twelve Is Enough," *New Republic*, May 14, 1990, p. 23.
4. *Seattle Post-Intelligencer*, November 7, 1991, p. A1.
5. Neal R. Pierce, "Zeroing in on Permanent Incumbency," *National Journal*, October 6, 1990, p. 2417.
6. Mary Collins, "News of the Congress by the Congress," *Washington Journalism Review*, June 1990, p. 30.
7. Ibid.
8. "An Elected Aristocracy," *Wall Street Journal*, November 6, 1990, p. A22.
9. Speech by Gov. Douglas Wilder at Virginia Commonwealth University, Richmond, Virginia, October 1, 1990.
10. "Terms of Limitation," *Wall Street Journal*, December 11, 1989, p. A14.
11. James Payne, "Bad Influence," *Reason*, August/September 1991.
12. Speech by Ralph Nader, University of Southern California, October 4, 1990.
13. Interview, May 2, 1992.
14. Kettering Foundation, Dayton, Ohio, June 1991.
15. Interview, May 3, 1992.
16. Speech by Larry Hansen, Joyce Foundation, February 18, 1992.

17. Interview, April 8, 1992.
18. Interview, February 15, 1991.
19. Jon Keller, "Throw the Bums Out," *Boston Phoenix*, March 29, 1991, p. 7.

## Chapter 2

1. Steve Bronsnan, "Alexander Uses Campaign Money for Personal Expenses," *Memphis Commercial Appeal*, April 23, 1992, p. A5.
2. Interview, April 7, 1992.
3. National Taxpayers Union study, April 1992.
4. Interview, February 6, 1992.

## Chapter 3

1. Congressional Research Service Report for Congress, March 16, 1989.
2. Ibid., p. 20.
3. National Survey of 1,000 Adults between March 28 and April 1, 1992, American Viewpoint, Inc., Alexandria, Virginia, p. 1.
4. Hendrick Hertzberg, "Twelve Is Enough," *New Republic*, May 14, 1990.
5. David C. Huckabee, "Reelection Rates of House Incumbents," CRS Report for Congress, 1989.
6. National Survey, op. cit.

## Chapter 4

1. Internal memorandum, National Republican Congressional Campaign Committee, April 1991.
2. James T. Bennett and Thomas J. DiLorenzo, *Official Lies: Federal Government Propaganda* (Alexandria, Va.: Groom Books, 1992), p. 62.
3. Ibid., p. 68.

## Chapter 5

1. Charles Mathesian, "Labor Allies Desert Kolter," *Congressional Quarterly*, April 15, 1992, p. 1019.

## Chapter 6

1. GAO Audit of House Office of the Sergeant-at-Arms, September 1991.
2. In accordance with 2 U.S.C. 81a (July 26, 1949).
3. "Congressman Bill Alexander Reports to the First District of Arkansas," March 1992 newletter, mailed at taxpayer expense to all the residents of his district.

## Chapter 7

1. Quoted in *Roll Call*, December 29, 1989, p. A1.
2. Interview, May 6, 1992.
3. Interview, April 8, 1992.
4. Interview, February 12, 1992.
5. Interview, January 6, 1992.
6. Tom Dunkel, "Quake in the Statehouse," *Insight*, May 18, 1992, p. 11.
7. Interview, January 18, 1992.
8. Interview, April 19, 1992.
9. Discussion with reporter Joe Klein, May 5, 1992.
10. Alan Ehrenhalt, *The United States of Ambition* (New York: Random House, 1991), p. 242–43.
11. Elizabeth Kantor, "Packing Their Bags," *Washington Post*, December 15, 1984, p. C1.
12. Interview, February 14, 1991.
13. Interview, March 6, 1991.
14. Remarks by Rep. James McDermott to a group of Washington lobbyists, June 19, 1991.
15. Survey by Charles Price, California State University at Chico.
16. Nelson W. Polsby, "Congress Bashing for Beginners," *The Public Interest*, Summer 1990, p. 20.

## Chapter 8

1. Farewell speech, Phoenix, Arizona, November 20, 1986.
2. Fritz Hollings, testifying before a Senate Appropriations subcommittee, April 21, 1975, p. 1241.
3. John L. Jackley, *Hill Rat* (Washington, D.C.:Regnery Gateway, 1992), p.13.
4. Interview, September 25, 1990.

5. Charles Babcock, "Interest Group Honoraria Plentiful for Top Hill Aides," *Washington Post*, October 6, 1989, p. A1.

6. "Influence as Usual," *Wall Street Journal*, December 3, 1990, p. A22.

7. Quoted in Hedrick Smith, *The Power Game* (New York:Random House, 1987), p. 283.

8. Interview, April 1, 1992.

9. Speech by Sen. Robert Kerrey, September 18, 1991.

10. Sen. Warren Rudman's press conference announcing his retirement, March 24, 1992.

11. Thomas J. DiLorenzo and James Bennett, *Official Lies: Federal Government Propaganda* (Alexandria, Va.: Groom Books, 1992), p. 169.

12. Dale van Atta, "Annunzio Should Look Before Leaping," *Washington Merry-go-round*, July 24, 1990.

13. U.S. Rep. Chuck Douglas, "Section 89: What Staff Hath Created, Congress Should Take Away," *Congressional Record*, May 24, 1989, p. E1853.

14. Interview, June 5, 1989.

15. Interview, March 23, 1991.

16. Ibid.

## Chapter 9

1. Mark Petracca, "Rotation in Office: The History of an Idea," paper prepared for a conference at the Rockefeller Institute of Government at SUNY-Albany, October 1991.

2. Robert Struble, Jr., and Z. W. Jahre, "Rotation in Office," *Political Science and Politics*, March 1991, p. 37.

3. Ed Crane, "Six and Twelve: The Case for Serious Term Limits," *National Civic Review*, Summer 1991, p. 250.

4. Edmund C. Burnett, *The Continental Congress* (New York: Macmillan, 1941), p. 250.

5. Ibid, p. 605–06.

6. Charles O. Jones, *Every Second Year* (Washington, D.C.: Brookings Institution, 1968), p. 4.

7. *The Life and Selected Writings of Thomas Jefferson* (New York: Random House, 1944), p. 19.

8. George F. Will, "Is 18 Years on the Hill Enough?" *Washington Post*, January 7, 1990, p. A22.

9. Charles R. Kesler, "The Case Against Congressional Term Limitations," *Policy Review*, Summer 1990, p. 21.

10. Mike Klein, "Limiting Congressional Terms," Americans to Limit Congressional Terms, 1989, p. 6.
11. Kesler, *Case Against* op. cit.
12. Nelson W. Polsby, *The Congressional Career* (New York: Random House, 1971), p. 23.
13. Rep. Bill McCollum, speech to the Conservative Political Action Conference, Washington, D.C., March 1, 1990.
14. "22nd Amendment," *Washington Post*, February 29, 1951.
15. Sula P. Richardson, *Congressional Tenure*, Congressional Research Service, September 13, 1990, p. 5.
16. Struble and Jahre, *Rotation*, op. cit.
17. Thad L. Beyle, "Term Limits for State Elected Executive Officials," paper prepared for a conference at the Rockefeller Institute of Government at SUNY-Albany, October 1991.
18. Janet Hook, "New Drive to Limit Tenure Revives an Old Proposal," *Congressional Quarterly*, February 24, 1990, p. 568.

## Chapter 10

1. Interview, February 14, 1991.
2. Interview, February 14, 1991.
3. Oliver Starr, Jr., *Twilight of the Imperial Congress* (Webster Groves, Mo.: Missourian Publishing Co., 1991), p. 17.
4. Interview, October 11, 1991.
5. Press Release from Rep. Jim Lightfoot, October 17, 1990.
6. Jon Keller, "Throw the Bums Out," *Boston Phoenix*, March 29, 1991, p. 7.
7. Interview, April 9, 1992.
8. Interview, November 16, 1991.
9. Karen Foerstel, "Tenure of Top Senate Aides Plummets," *Roll Call*, December 9, 1991, p. 1.
10. Text of Proposition 140, California Secretary of State voter pamphlet, November 1990.
11. Interview, August 8, 1991.
12. Interview, August 2, 1991.
13. James Payne, *The Culture of Spending* (San Francisco: Institute for Contemporary Studies, 1991), p. 181.
14. Stuart Rothenberg, "Term Limits," *Nation's Business*, January 1992, p. 21.

15. Speech to Citizens for Congressional Reform, San Jose, Calif., December 11, 1990.
16. New Orleans City Clerk's report, October 1991.
17. Campaign literature of Freedom, Inc., October 1990.
18. News conference, January 6, 1992.
19. Ibid.
20. Norman Leahy, "Turnover and the Case for Term Limits," *U.S. Term Limits* publication, May 1992, p. 1.
21. Interview, October 9, 1990.
22. Interview, October 20, 1990.

## Chapter 11

1. Thomas F. Hartnett, "Put Members of Congress on a Short Lease," *Wall Street Journal*, September 19, p. A14.
2. Letter to James K. Coyne, August 8, 1989.
3. Paul English, "Bellmon Supports Limits on Legislative Service," *Daily Oklahoman*, July 12, 1990, p. A4.
4. Steve Lockmeyer, "Walters Backs Limiting Terms," *Daily Oklahoman*, May 31, 1990, p. A10.
5. Dan Walters, *Fresno Bee*, June 9, 1990, p. A6.
6. John H. Fund, "Four Days to Term Limit Tuesday," *Wall Street Journal*, November 2, 1990, p. A14.
7. Ibid.
8. Pacific Legal Foundation memorandum, January 11, 1991.
9. "Proposition 140 Fallout," *California Journal*, December 1990, p. 17.
10. Interview, December 15, 1990.
11. Interview, December 14, 1990.
12. Interview, February 28, 1991.
13. Editorial, *Los Angeles Daily News*, October 25, 1990, p. A18.
14. Interview, October 30, 1990.
15. Pacific Legal Foundation memorandum, March 2, 1991.
16. Interview, February 2, 1991.
17. Preliminary polling by Celinda Lake showed that over 70 percent of Washington State voters backed term limits. Will Robinson and David Dixon, "How We Short-Circuited the Terminators," *Campaign* magazine, February 1992.
18. Quoted in the *Orange County Register*, November 12, 1991, p. A17.
19. Transcript of "Capitol Newsbeat" debate between Rep. Al Swift and Ed Crane of the Cato Institute, November 2, 1991.

## Chapter 12

1. CBS Evening News, November 1, 1991.
2. Janet Beales, "Washington State's Term Limit Fever," *Wall Street Journal*, September 18, 1991, p. A20.
3. The Kamber Group, "Modern Day Snake Oil: Term Limitations and Why They Must Be Defeated," October 1991, p. 51.
4. Interview, October 11, 1991.
5. Interview, December 21, 1991.
6. Interview, July 11, 1991.
7. Interview, May 2, 1991.
8. Ibid.
9. Interview, October 30, 1991.
10. Quoted in *Emerge* magazine, January 1991.
11. Interview, October 11, 1991.
12. "Term Limits Are a Tonic for Democracy," *Albany Times and Herald*, September 25, 1991, p. A9.
13. Interview, November 2, 1991.
14. Interview, October 31, 1991.
15. Hendrik Hertzberg, "Twelve Is Enough," *New Republic*, May 14, 1990, p. 23.
16. Ellen Goodman, "Congress Is Changing—And That's Good," *Philadelphia Inquirer*, April 14, 1991, p. A11.
17. Editorial, WCVB-TV, October 8, 1991.
18. Interview, November 1, 1991.
19. Interview, February 1, 1991.
20. Interview, February 14, 1991.
21. Speech to U.S. Term Limits Conference, Boston, Massachusetts, May 2, 1992.

## Chapter 13

1. CBS Evening News, November 1, 1991.
2. Quoted in *Wall Street Journal*, October 13, 1991, p. A21.
3. Interview, April 13, 1991.
4. Internal memorandum by William Mellor and Jonathan Emord, Institute for Justice, Washington, D.C., September 1991.
5. Stephen Glazier, "Each State Can Limit Re-Election to Congress," *Wall Street Journal*, June 19, 1990, p. A14.
6. Interview, December 13, 1991.

7. Ronald D. Elving, "National Drive to Limit Terms Casts Shadow Over Congress," *Congressional Quarterly*, October 26, 1991, p. 3103.
8. Ibid., see footnote 3.
9. Lawrence Tribe, *American Constitutional Law*, 2nd ed. (New York: Saint Martin's Press, 1986), p. 1097.
10. Thomas E. Cronin, *Direct Democracy: The Politics of Initiative, Referendum and Recall* (Cambridge, Mass.: Harvard University Press, 1989), p. 25.
11. Interview, September 23, 1991.
12. Ibid., see footnote 5.

## Chapter 14

1. Interview, June 13, 1990.
2. Interview, September 23, 1991.
3. Interview, September 19, 1991.
4. Interview, February 12, 1992.

# Appendix

# FIFTY STATE REPORT ON TERM LIMIT ACTIVITY

There are three national organizations working to implement term limits:

Americans to Limit Congressional Terms. The first and largest term-limits organization with over 300,000 members. Founded in 1989 by James K. Coyne, the co-author of this book, and 32 other former Congressmen. ALCT can be reached at 1050 Langley Hill Drive, Langley, VA 22101. 1-(800)-6IS-ENUF or (800) 647-3683.

Americans Back in Charge was founded in 1990 by Terry Considine, the author of Colorado's term limit law. It provides support services for grass-roots term limits around the country. Its adjunct office, the Term Limits Legal Institute in Washington, D.C., helps defend term-limit initiatives in court. Americans Back in Charge is located at 1873 S. Bellaire, Suite 1700, Denver, Colorado 80222 (303) 758-7343, 758-7073 fax.

U.S. Term Limits was established in 1991 to restore citizen control of government by rallying Americans to limit congressional, state and local terms. U.S. Term Limits can be reached at 666 11th Street, N.W., Suite 840, Washington, D.C. 20001. (800) 733-6440.

**Alabama**—Bill introduced in legislature. Group forming to lobby and seek term limit pledges from 1992 candidates.

David Donaldson
P.O. Box 530390
Birmingham, AL 35253
(205) 877-3021

Dean Wilson
815 Union St.
Selma, AL 36701
(205) 875-6214

**Alaska**—Anchorage voter initiative was successful in limiting terms for municipal offices. Groups working for separate state and federal 1994 initiatives.

*State Group*
Alaskans for Legislative
  Reform
P.O. Box 242592
Anchorage, AK 99524-2592
(907) 561-1265/562-7839
Fax (907) 561-7531
Contact: Jay Loesch/Bob Bell

*Federal Group*
Fritz Pettyjohn
P.O. Box 110912
Anchorage, AK 99511
(907) 345-5174

**Arizona**—Initiative certified for 1992 ballot. Federal limits are 6 years in U.S. House. Arizona State House of Representatives has passed term limit amendment with 12 year U.S. House limit. No action yet taken by the State Senate.

Citizens for Limited Terms
4700 N. Central Ave.
  Suite 121
Phoenix, AZ 85012
(602) 274-2020
Contact: Bill Long

Arizona C.C.R.
P.O. Box 11707
Prescott, AZ 86304
(602) 445-0874
Contact: Al Walther

**Arkansas**—Petition drive underway for 1992 ballot. Limits state-wide offices, state legislature and U.S. Congress (6 year U.S. House limit). Legislative effort was killed in committee in 1991.

Arkansas for Governmental
  Reform
P.O. Box 1447
Little Rock, AR 72203
In state (800) 489-1992,
  (501) 661-8699
Contact: Steve Munn/
  Skip Cook

**California**—Proposition 140 leader Pete Schabarum is leading the campaign to limit Congress (6 years in the U.S. House). Initiative has won ballot certification.

Limit Congress
880 W. First Street, #612
Los Angeles, CA 90012
(213) 617-3874, fax 620-0993
Contact: Pete Schabarum

Additional contacts:

ACTIV (also active in efforts
    to place a None of the
    Above line on ballots)
9083 Sequel Drive #2
Aptos, CA 95003
(408) 688-8986, fax 662-9138
Contact: Lee Phelps

**Colorado**—State and federal limits passed in 1990 with 71% of the vote. (Colorado Springs, Littleton, and Loveland have passed limits on city officials.)

Sen. Terry Considine
1700 Lincoln Street
    Suite 4706
Denver, CO 80203
(303) 757-2567, fax 757-3841

**Connecticut**—Four resolutions have been introduced in the state legislature. Groups forming now to lobby and seek term limit pledges from 1992 candidates.

Alexander T. Van Rensselaer
Connecticut Citizens for
    Congressional Reform
1071 Post Road East
Westport, CT 06880
(203) 221-0100, fax 454-4923

**Delaware**—A bill has been introduced in the legislature.

**Florida**—Initiative limiting state and federal terms is certified. Limits U.S. House to 8 years. Defeated court challenge by politicians to keep them off the ballot—The Florida Legislature is considering a similar Constitutional amendment but with longer terms—12 years—in the U.S. House. (City term limits were passed in Jacksonville 82% to 18% in 1991.)

Eight is Enough!
P.O. Box 4888
Orlando, FL 32802
(407) 839-5888, fax 839-4360
Contact: Phil Handy/
    John Sowinski

**Georgia**—Number of bills have been introduced in the legislature.

Georgians to Limit
    Congressional Terms
P.O. Box 742
Dalton, GA 30722
(404) 278-6514
Contact: Glen Hicks

**Hawaii**—Bill introduced to limit state legislators to 8 years.

State Representative
    Jane Tatibouet
235 So. Beretania St.
    Room 1109
Honolulu, HI 96813
(808) 586-6470

**Idaho**—Resolution calling on Congress to pass a constitutional amendment passed the state Senate and House and was signed by the Governor of 3/31/92. A group is petitioning for a federal initiative (8 year limit in U.S. House), and separate legislation is being lobbied for on the state level.

*Federal*
Citizens for Political
    Reform (CPR)
P.O. Box 836
Boise, ID 83701
(208) 336-4449
Contact: Roland Smith

*State*
Idahoans for
    Competitive Government
701 West Franklin St.
Boise, ID 83702
(208) 342-6000
Contact: Dwight Johnson

**Illinois**—A state term limit group is petitioning for a 1994 initiative limiting state legislators. State initiative process prohibits a federal limit initiative.

Robert Redfern
508 West Main
Fairfield, IL 62837
(618) 842-3644
fax (618) 842-7246

Taxpayer's Coalition for a
   2-Term Limit
23 West, 546 Pine Drive
Wheaton, IL 60188
(708) 462-2062
Contact: Faye Smith

**Indiana**—Group forming to lobby and pursue term limit pledges for 1992 candidates.

Don Clay
3213 Eden Drive
Bloomington, IN 47401
(812) 333-7258

Tim Deatrick
Hoosiers for Better Gov't.
521 Navajo Drive
New Albany, IN 47150
(812) 944-6100

**Iowa**—A Senate Joint Resolution has been introduced and is in committee.

Tenure Limit on Congress
P.O. Box 674
Burlington, IA 52601-0674
Contact: Fred Meeker

**Kansas**—City of Wichita passed term limits. Resolutions have been introduced in state legislature. Group has formed to lobby.

Kansans for Term Limits
3101 SW MacVicar, #102A
Topeka, KS 66611
(913) 267-4173
Contact: Jim Van Slyke

**Kentucky**—Legislation has been introduced in 1992 session. Group formed to campaign to get candidates to pledge their support for term limits.

State Representative
 Jo Elizabeth Bryant
P.O. Box 536
Williamsburg, KY 40769
(502) 564-8100

**Louisiana**—New Orleans overwhelmingly passed city council limits. Three bills have been introduced in the state Senate and three in the House. A group has formed to push for state and federal limits.

Louisiana '96
1 Seine Court, Suite 200
New Orleans, LA 70114
(504) 364-0112
Contact: Peter Devine

**Maine**—Initiative language has been drawn up and is expected to be filed this year. They then have a year period to collect 52,278 signatures for the 1994 ballot. Group is prepared to sue the Secretary of State who has previously tried to block term limit petition efforts.

Mainers Back in Charge
27 Danforth Street
Norway, ME 04268
(207) 743-9219 or 743-9228
Contact: Sharon Bouchard

**Maryland**—Bill introduced in legislature. Groups have formed to pursue county-wide term limit initiatives, pledges from '92 candidates, and lobby the state legislature. Non-binding initiative passed in Rockville, MD for term limits on the city council.

Marylanders to Limit
 Congressional Terms
799 Dividing Road
Severna Park, MD 21146
(410) 544-3326
Contact: Bob Schaeffer

**Massachusetts**—LIMITS collected over 72,000 valid signatures to send a Constitutional Amendment to the state legislature. Amendment limits state and federal terms (8 years in U.S. House.) Now the amendment must get at least a 25% vote from the full legislature on two occasions in order to be placed on the 1994 ballot. Governor and 3 other statewide elected officials have endorsed term limits. Legislature has thus far been making procedural maneuvers to avoid a vote on the amendment.

LIMITS
P.O. Box 2432
Worcester, MA 01613
(413) 477-0900
Contact: Dorothea Vitrac

**Michigan**—Initiative has been certified for the 1992 ballot. Limits apply to state-wide officials, state legislature, and U.S. Congress (House limits are 6 years). Jay Van Andel of Amway Corporation and Paul McCracken, former chairman of the President's Council of Economic Advisors, are co-chairs of the campaign.

Campaign to Limit
  Politicians' Terms
4616 44th Street, SE
Grand Rapids, MI 49512
In state: (800) 272-1011
(616) 957-2177, fax 957-2394
Contact: Tim Purdy,
  Tish Berkey

**Minnesota**—A constitutional amendment has been introduced in the House and 2 bills (S.F. 227 and S.F. 916) have been introduced in the Senate. Governor Arne Carlson has endorsed term limits.

Minnesotans for Term Limits
1900 Foshay Tower
Minneapolis, MN 55402
(612) 337-5536
Contact: Ben Whitney

**Mississippi**—Four separate bills have been introduced in the 1992 session.

Contact:  Robert Green
     Rt. 2, Box 20-A
     Ripley, MS 38663
     (601) 837-4596

**Missouri**—Separate initiatives on the state and federal level have been filed and petitions are being circulated. The U.S. House limit is 8 years. The group has the support of U.S. Rep. Mel Hancock (R-Springfield). In 1990, Kansas City approved city-wide term limits, 57% in favor.

Missourians for Limited
  Terms
P.O. Box 317
Marshfield, MO 65706
(417) 468-3074
In state: (800) 473-TERM
Contact: John Thompson


**Montana**—A group is collecting signatures for a 1992 initiative. State Rep. Fred Thomas is the author of the measure. (House is a 6 year limit). Governor Stan Stephens has endorsed term limits.

Citizens for CI-64
707 Tower
Helena, MT 59601
(406) 443-3797
Contact: Riley Johnson


**Nebraska**—Group is petitioning to place an initiative on the 1992 ballot (8 year House limit).

Nebraskans for Term Limits
P.O. Box 57193
Lincoln, NE 68505
(402) 333-2912
Contact: Ed Jaksha


**Nevada**—Group petitioning for amendment limiting terms of their federal delegation (6 years in the U.S. House). Amendment will go on the 1992 ballot, and if passed, must be passed again in 1994.

Nevadans for Term Limits
5715 N. Balsam Road
Las Vegas, NV 89130
(702) 658-2112, 658-2090
Contact: Hal Schuster

**New Hampshire**—Two bills were introduced in 1991. Former U.S. Senator Gordon Humphrey is working on new legislation.

Sen. Gordon Humphrey
P.O. Box 1461, State House
Concord, NH 03301
(603) 798-4274, fax 798-5274

**New Jersey**—Group has formed to lobby (a virtually new legislature after '91 election) and implement term limit pledge program for 1992 congressional candidates.

REVOLT
P.O. Box 989
Brick, NJ 08723
(908) 892-1518
Contact: Tom Blomquist

**New Mexico**—Resolutions introduced in both House and Senate. State Rep. Mark Caruso leads the legislative battle.

New Mexico Citizens for
  Term Limits
P.O. Box 35367
Albuquerque, NM 87176
(505) 291-8585
Contact: Greg Zanetti

**New York**—Two bills have been introduced. The Empire State Foundation in Albany has done a study supportive of term limitation.

*Bill Sponsors*
Assemblyman
  Richard Coombe
(518) 455-5355
Room 322
Legislative Office Bldg.
Albany, NY 12248

**North Carolina**—Two bills introduced in Senate. Group being organized to lobby and solicit term limit pledges from candidates.

Louis T. March
Allen Commercial
Dean Witter Building
4700 Homewood Court
Raleigh, NC 27609
(919) 781-1100
fax (919) 781-1118

North Carolina Term Limits
6204 Oak Burr Court
Pleasant Garden, NC 27313
(919) 674-8955
Contact: Al Coggan

**North Dakota**—Bills introduced in Senate and House. Separate initiatives being filed to limit terms on state and federal level. (12 years in U.S. House)

North Dakotans for Better
  Government
P.O. Box 2074
Bismarck, ND 58502
(701) 255-1705
Contact: Kent French

**Ohio**—Petition certified for the 1992 ballot. Limits state-wide officials, state legislature and U.S. Congress (8 years in the House).

Ohioans for Term Limits
12500 Elmwood Avenue
Cleveland, OH 44111
(216) 871-6481
Contact: John Jazwa

**Oregon**—Initiative certified for 1992 ballot. Limits apply to both state and federal officials (6 year limit in U.S. House).

LIMITS
19201 SE Division, Suite C
Gresham, OR 97030
(503) 667-8315 or 665-4142
fax (503) 667-4948
Contact: Frank Eisenzimmer

**Oklahoma**—Passed state-wide limits in 1990 with 67% of the vote. Considering initiative on federal limits—probably in 1994.

Lloyd Noble, III
324 Main Street, Suite 612
Tulsa, OK 74103
(918) 584-0612
  fax (918) 599-7167

**Pennsylvania**—Group forming to lobby for term limits.

Pennsylvanians for Term
  Limits
RD 5, Box 156
Blairsville, PA 15717
(412) 244-4081 w/459-8247 h
Contact: Mike Boland

**Rhode Island**—Two bills introduced in 1991 legislative session. Governor Sundlun supports term limits and is preparing his own bill for 1992.

**South Carolina**—Bills are in committee as 1992 session begins. Group has formed to lobby and has been collecting petition signatures to demonstrate support.

South Carolinians for Term               also:
  Limits
c/o A Better Connection                  616 Harbor Creek Drive
1042 N. Pleasantburg Drive               Charleston SC 29412
Greenville, SC 29607                     (803) 795-3118
(803) 235-3211                           Contact: Carter Hardwick
Contact: Wes Drawdy

**South Dakota**—Resolution passed in 1990 requesting that the U.S. Congress take action to limit terms. Initiative certified for the 1992 ballot. Effort is being led by Jeff Hayzlett and St. Rep. John Timmer. Initiative limits state legislators and constitutional officers to 8 years and the U.S. House and Senate members to 12 years.

South Dakotans for Limited
  Terms
P.O. Box 1684
Sioux Falls, SD 57101
(605) 338-6621
Contact: Jeff Hayzlett

**Tennessee**—Four resolutions have been introduced for a constitutional amendment. Statewide group formed to lobby.

Citizens to Limit Political
  Terms
P.O. Box 204
Manchester, TN 37355
(615) 728-3861
Contact: James Herbert
  Threet


**Texas**—State lobbying group is collecting signatures to demonstrate massive grassroots support for the issue. Non-binding vote in '92 GOP Primary gained 86% in favor of term limits of 6 years in U.S. House and 12 years in Senate. (San Antonio has passed term limitation for city officials. Houston passed city-wide term limit initiative at 1991 general election.) Governor Ann Richards, a Democrat, has endorsed term limits.

Texans for Term Limitation
P.O. Box 1906
Houston, TX 77251
(713) 546-2545
Contact: Rob Mosbacher


**Utah**—Petition drive underway for 1994 ballot initiative. Initiative limits county officials, state legislature and Congress (8 years).

Term Limits
50 West 7200 South
Midvale, UT 84047
(801) 966-3252
Contact: John Bullock


**Vermont**—Proposed constitutional amendment still in the State House. Former Governor Madeleine Kunin has come out in favor of term limits.

Timothy Philbin
P.O. Box 813
Rutland, VT 05702
(802) 775-2311


**Virginia**—Lobbying group has formed.

Virginians for Political
  Reform
P.O. Box 14829
Richmond, VA 23221
(804) 353-4554
Contact: Joseph Vasapoli,
  Mark Hagood

**Washington**—Petition drive underway to place initiative 573 on 1992
ballot. Previous initiative was rewritten to take out retroactive clause.
(Lost 46% to 54% on 1991 retroactive initiative.)

LIMIT
P.O. Box 98003
Tacoma, WA 98498
(206) 759-1212
  fax (206) 759-3602
Contact: Sherry Bockwinkel

**West Virginia**—Group formed to lobby legislature for term limits and
initiative/referendum. State Sen. Mark Manchin introduced legislation
to limit legislative terms in 1991.

Concerned Citizens of
  West Virginia
101 Laurel Ridge Road
Scott Depot, WV 25560
(304) 757-7224
Contact: Viloris or Lou Allen

**Wisconsin**—Three Constitutional Amendments were introduced in
the legislature. Badgers Back in Charge will seek new legislation action
in 1993 session. They need legislative approval in two successive legislative sessions, and a majority vote of the public.

Badgers Back in Charge
P.O. Box 1992
Freedom, WI 54131
(715) 693-3018
Contact: Kevin Hermening

**Wyoming**—Certified for 1992 ballot. Initiative will limit state-wide officials, state legislators, and Congress. Limit is 6 years for U.S. House. (Bill in Senate died in committee in 1991.)

> Wyomingites for Citizen
>   Government
> P.O. Box 4322
> Casper, WY 82604
> (307) 237-4648 or 674-4983
> Contact: Dave Dawson /
>   Jack Adsit

**District of Columbia**—Initiative petition drive underway to place the issue before the voters in 1992. Limits Mayor, City Council and Board of Education to 2 four-year terms; Advisory Neighborhood Council to 3 two-year terms.

> D.C. Term Limits Committee
> 121 Raleigh Street, S.E.
> Washington, D.C. 20032
> (202) 562-4974
> Contact: R. Calvin Lockridge

# INDEX